STATE v. BURNS

Problems and Case File

1998 NITA EDUCATIONAL SERVICES COMMITTEE

NITA

STATE v. BURNS

Problems and Case File

by

Anthony J. Bocchino
Professor of Law
Temple University

Donald Beskind
Attorney at Law
Chapel Hill, North Carolina

REVISED FIFTH EDITION

1992

Reproduction Permission
National Institute for Trial Advocacy
1602 North Ironwood
South Bend, Indiana 46635
(800) 225-6482
Fax (574) 271-8375
E-mail nita.1@nd.edu

Bocchino, A. and D. Beskind, *State v. Burns,* Revised Fifth Edition (1992).

ISBN 1-55681-297-3

4/96

Section I

Problems

STATE v. BURNS PROBLEMS

TABLE OF CONTENTS

Page

Introduction P-1

Method of Instruction P-3

Direct, Cross, and Redirect Examination P-5
1. James Carletti P-7
2. Arthur Hellman P-7
3. Mary Burns P-8
4. Laurence Roberts P-8

Handling and Introduction of Exhibits P-9
5. Gun P-13
6. Newspaper P-14
7. Gun Registrations P-14

Use of Visual Aids P-15
8. Chalkboard and Diagram P-17
9. Diagram P-17

Impeachment and Rehabilitation P-19
10. Lauren Jones P-21
11. Mary Burns P-21
12. John Burns P-22

Adverse Examination P-23
13. Laurence Roberts P-25
14. Mary Burns P-25

Witness Preparation P-27
15. Lauren Jones P-27
16. John Burns P-28
17. Arthur Hellman P-28

Advanced Direct and Cross Examination P-29
18. John Burns P-29
19. Lauren Jones P-29
20. James Carletti P-30

Page

Jury Selection P-31
21. Problem P-32

Opening Statements P-35
22. Problem P-37

Closing Arguments P-39
23. Problem P-40

INTRODUCTION

The problems in this book are intended to simulate realistic courtroom situations. Advance preparation is essential to their successful utilization as instructional materials.

These problems refer to *State v. Burns*, one of the case files in NITA's *Problems and Cases in Trial Advocacy,* CLE Edition, series. These case files have been designed to simulate the materials a trial lawyer would have on the eve of trial. The materials must be mastered before attempting to perform the problems in a courtroom setting.

All years in these materials are stated in the following form:

* YR-0 indicates the actual year in which the case is being tried (i.e., the present year);
* YR-1 indicates the next preceding year (please use the actual year);
* YR-2 indicates the second preceding year (please use the actual year); etc.

At the outset we should acknowledge that it is impossible for one person to teach another how to become a trial lawyer. Advocacy is an art, the performance of which is dependent on talent and mastery of skills. One becomes a trial lawyer through a mixture of predisposition, motivation, observation, doing it, reading how others have done it and then constantly repeating the latter three — doing, observing, and reading.

It is possible, however, to simulate some of the intellectual, ethical, emotional and physical demands of trial lawyering and advocacy teaching in a mock courtroom or classroom setting. That is what is done at the National Institute for Trial Advocacy. These materials are intended to serve as the basic teaching materials for trial advocacy courses and programs that are based upon the learning-by-doing method. Although the materials have been prepared especially for NITA programs, they are adaptable for use in other settings.

Most of the skills learned in a trial advocacy course will be applicable to trial work generally, without regard to the nature of the case. Obviously, however, different kinds of cases present different problems. We believe that these materials illustrate some of the more significant peculiarities of a murder and robbery trial.

The student should read the assigned case file as soon as possible. A reading of the complete case file early will permit the student to fit an individual problem into the context of the entire litigation. The student should then read the assigned problems and do as much preparation as possible in advance of the program. Preparation time during the program will be limited. Thus, advance preparation will allow a more efficient use of the limited time available during the program.

P-2

State v. Burns Problems

METHOD OF INSTRUCTION

NITA programs, and other learning-by-doing programs, have certain unique characteristics to which these materials are particularly suited. These programs typically use teaching teams comprised of law teachers, practicing trial lawyers and judges. The programs are highly intensive, all-day sessions lasting from five to sixteen working days. All make substantial use of videotape to record student performances for later playback and critique.

These materials also are adaptable for the more typical law school program in which classes are spread out over a semester, teaching teams are unavailable and videotape may not be feasible. The following are some ideas for use of the materials whether they are used at an intensive NITA-type session or in a longer law school program.

It is contemplated that the materials will be used in a simulated courtroom session. A judge, whether actual or portrayed, will preside at the front of the classroom. A student lawyer will be called on to begin the problem. The examining lawyer will be opposed by an adversary, who will be portrayed by another member of the class or, when a teaching team is available, by a visiting lawyer. The witness will have been prepared and will respond to a proper examination. The lawyer may complete the examination or be interrupted so that another lawyer can continue the examination. Several lawyers may be called on to represent both sides before the problem is exhausted and the next problem begun.

At a NITA session, a section of twenty-four students will remain together for two hours to work on a series of problems. The section then ordinarily will split into two or three smaller groups. The students will continue to work on the problems in these groups.

During the course of any presentation by a student, whether in large or small groups, another lawyer may be called on to substitute for the participating lawyer. The substituting lawyer may pick up where the other left off or, with permission of the instructor, may begin again. In short, the students may be called on at any time to undertake an assigned examination.

Many teachers require universal preparation; each student must be prepared to perform at least one side of each problem.

P-4
State v. Burns Problems

DIRECT, CROSS AND REDIRECT EXAMINATION

The ability to examine and oppose the examination of witnesses in open court in an adversary setting is the most basic skill of the trial lawyer. Yet, the most common criticism of trial lawyers is that they are unable to conduct proper, intelligent and purposeful examinations and to oppose these examinations.

As with any skill, practice is the only sure way to achievement. The practice should be conducted with some guidelines in mind.

1. The purpose of any witness examination is to elicit information.

2. The basic format is an interrogative dialogue.

3. The witness is probably insecure. He or she is appearing in a strange environment and is expected to perform under strange rules. This is a handicap you must overcome on direct and an advantage you have (and may choose to exploit) on cross.

4. Your questions should be short, simple and understandable to the witness, the judge and the jury on both direct and cross examination.

   (a) It is imperative that your audience — the judge and the jury — understand your question so that they reasonably can anticipate and comprehend the answer.

   (b) On direct examination the insecurity or anxieties of the witness will be increased if he or she does not understand your questions.

   (c) On cross examination the complex argumentative question provides a refuge for the witness to evade the point.

5. As a general proposition, you may not lead on direct except as to preliminary matters or to refresh the recollection of the witness. Both of these exceptions are discretionary with the judge.

6. In any event, on direct examination leading questions and the perfunctory answers they elicit are not persuasive.

7. On cross examination you may lead and you should do so. Control of the witness on cross is imperative.

8. At the outset of direct examination, have the witness introduce himself or herself. Then, place him or her in the controversy on trial, and elicit the who, where, when, what, how and why of the relevant information the witness has to offer. Then quit. Do not be repetitious.

9. If you know that the cross examination will elicit unfavorable information, consider the possible advantage of eliciting it during your direct examination.

10. Do not conduct a cross examination that does nothing other than afford the witness an opportunity to repeat his or her direct testimony.

    (a) If there is nothing to be gained by cross examination, waive it.

    (b) If you can accomplish something by cross examination, get to it. Organize your points and make them.

    (c) Be cautious about cross examining on testimony elicited on direct that was favorable to your position. You may lose it.

    (d) Be cautious about asking a question to which you do not know or cannot reasonably anticipate the answer. Be particularly cautious in those situations in which the only evidence on the point will be the unknown answer.

11. Listen to (do not assume) the answers of the witness. As an examiner on either direct or cross examination, you are entitled to responsive answers. Insist on them by a gentle nudge on direct or a motion to strike on cross (unless, of course, the answer is favorable, in which event accept it and return to the pending question).

12. Objections to the form of the question must be made before an answer is given. If the question reveals that the answer sought will be inadmissible, an objection must precede the answer. The grounds of the objection should be succinctly and specifically stated. If the question does not reveal the potential inadmissibility of the answer, but the answer is inadmissible, a prompt motion to strike should be succinctly and specifically stated. Only the interrogator is entitled to move to strike an answer on the *sole* ground that it was unresponsive to the question. If the answer is unresponsive *and* contains objectionable matter, then the opposing counsel is entitled to object.

13. If an objection to the content of the answer (e.g., relevancy, hearsay, etc.) as opposed to the form of the question, is sustained, then the interrogator should consider the need for an offer of proof at the first available opportunity. If an objection to the form of the question is sustained, then the interrogator should rephrase the question to cure the objection.

PROBLEM 1

James Carletti

Assume that the case is at trial, and the state's first witness is James Carletti.

(a) For the state, conduct a direct examination of Mr. Carletti.

(b) For the defendant, conduct a cross examination of Mr. Carletti.

(c) For the state, conduct any necessary redirect examination.

PROBLEM 2

Arthur Hellman

Assume that the case is at trial, and the state has called James Carletti and Lauren Jones. The state's next witness is Officer Arthur Hellman. For purposes of this problem, Hellman is to be examined on any aspects of his investigation except his identification of the fingerprints on the gun seized from the defendant.

(a) For the state, conduct a direct examination of Officer Hellman.

(b) For the defendant, conduct a cross examination of Officer Hellman.

(c) For the state, conduct any necessary redirect examination.

PROBLEM 3

Mary Burns

Assume that the case is at trial, the state has presented its case, and the defendant's motion for a judgment of acquittal has been denied. The defendant's first witness is Mary Burns.

(a) For the defendant, conduct a direct examination of Mrs. Burns.

(b) For the state, conduct a cross examination of Mrs. Burns.

(c) For the defendant, conduct any necessary redirect examination.

PROBLEM 4

Lawrence Roberts

Assume that the case is at trial, the state has presented its case, and the defendant's motion for a judgment of acquittal has been denied. Assume further that Mary Burns has testified for the defense. The defendant's next witness is Lawrence Roberts.

(a) For the defendant, conduct a direct examination of Mr. Roberts.

(b) For the state, conduct a cross examination of Mr. Roberts.

(c) For the defendant, conduct any necessary redirect examination.

HANDLING AND INTRODUCTION OF EXHIBITS

The ability to examine and oppose the examination of witnesses in open court in an adversary setting is the *most basic* skill of the trial lawyer.

The second basic skill of the trial lawyer is the proper, efficient and orderly handling and introduction of tangible evidence. Again, however, a common criticism of the trial bar is its lack of facility in this truly simple undertaking.

This is all the more regrettable when one considers the highly persuasive quality of relevant exhibits. Jurors (and judges, too) trust them. They are the real thing. They do not exaggerate as witnesses do and they do not overstep their bounds as lawyers do. Many a case has been won or lost because a particularly intriguing exhibit was received in evidence or excluded.

The four touchstones for the handling and introduction of exhibits are:

1. Authenticity
2. Relevance
3. The Hearsay Rule
4. The Best Evidence Rule

These four touchstones must be satisfied before an exhibit can be received in evidence. Some call it "laying the foundation." By whatever phrase, the essential element is testimony establishing that the exhibit is authentic and relevant and complies with both the hearsay and best evidence rules.

Authenticity is simply a demonstration that the exhibit is what it purports to be. Is this thing — whatever it is — that is being offered in evidence, *prima facie* that which it purports to be?[*] The essential requirement is testimonial vouching for the thing unless, of course, authenticity is established by admissions in the pleadings, discovery, or a request to admit. See, for example, Federal Rule of Civil Procedure 36.

Relevance, as well as the hearsay and best evidence rules, is intrinsically dependent on the issues raised in the case and the purpose for which the exhibit is offered in evidence. In each instance, however, the foundation must be laid demonstrating that the exhibit is relevant and that it complies with the hearsay and best evidence rules.

For each exhibit, counsel should check the four touchstones and then lay the foundation necessary for its admission in evidence through the testimony of one or more witnesses.

---

[*]The standard is a *prima facie* showing of authenticity, as the court determines admissibility. The weight to be assigned to the particular piece of evidence is left to the fact-finder.

As in the case of witness examination, the skill of handling and introducing exhibits is developed by practice and is conducted with certain guidelines in mind.

1. Select with care the witness or witnesses you will use to lay the foundation for your exhibits. A mistake here could be fatal.

2. Because the introduction of exhibits usually is done through witnesses, keep in mind the basic principles of witness examination.

3. Have the exhibit marked for identification by the appropriate court official (usually the court reporter or clerk) at the earliest opportunity. Many lawyers have their exhibits marked for identification prior to trial in the sequence in which they expect to use them. Some judges insist on this. It is a good practice in cases involving many exhibits. But also consider the advantages to be gained from a brief pause (respite for the witness) and a little bit of the lawyer doing his or her "thing" that attends your stepping to the bench and requesting in a voice the jury can hear, "Your Honor, may the reporter mark this document (or object) defendant's exhibit 1 for identification?"

4. Once the exhibit has been marked for identification, include that identification in any reference you make to the exhibit and see to it that your opponent, the witnesses, and the judge do likewise. Never permit the record to read merely, "this letter" or "that bottle" or "the photograph," etc.

5. Proceed to "lay the foundation" as follows:

   (a) Elicit from the authenticating witness those facts that qualify him or her to authenticate the exhibit. For example, have the witness say he saw the gun in the robber's hand.

   (b) Have the witness identify the exhibit by saying, for example, that State's Exhibit 1 is the gun (or looks like the gun) the witness saw in the robber's hand.

   (c) If the condition of the exhibit is a factor in its relevancy, either elicit testimony that its condition has not changed between the event and the time of trial, or offer a testimonial explanation of the change in condition.

   (d) If the exhibit is a reproduction of a place, a thing or an event (e.g., a photograph or a tape recording), elicit testimony that it fairly and accurately portrays that which it purports to portray.

   (e) If more than one witness is required to authenticate or connect the exhibit, withhold your offer until you have completed your foundation. A premature offer and rejection can condition a judge to reject the exhibit later when the foundation has been completed.

6. Once the foundation for an exhibit has been laid properly, offer it in evidence and obtain a ruling on its admissibility. In some jurisdictions an exhibit may not be offered during cross examination, and in those instances the formal offer of the exhibit is reserved to your case in chief or rebuttal.

7. When you are opposing the introduction of an exhibit, you are entitled to conduct a cross examination on the foundation before the court rules on the offer. The scope of this cross examination, often referred to as a voir dire on the exhibit, is limited to the admissibility of the exhibit. The proponent of the exhibit should be alert to so limit the voir dire on the exhibit and not permit the opponent to conduct a general cross examination on the weight that is to be given to the exhibit.

8. When you are opposing the introduction of exhibits, be on the alert for changed conditions and distortions (particularly in photographs). Insist that an adequate testimonial explanation of the changes be given by the authenticating witness.

9. Do not permit your opponent to display tangible items in the presence of the jury until they are marked for identification and proffered to the witness for identification.

10. Keep a separate record of the status of your exhibits and those of your opponent. Know at all times their identification numbers, their general descriptions, the witness or witnesses who authenticated them, and whether they have been offered and received or excluded. Many lawyers keep a columnar record somewhat like this:

Plaintiff's Exhibits

No.	Description	Witness	Date/Page of record offered	Date/Page of record received	Date/Page of record refused
1.	Letter from Jones	Smith	6/1/88 p. 138	6/1/88 p. 140	
2.	Hammer	Jones	6/2/88 p. 100		6/2/88 p. 210

11. At the close of your case, if you are uncertain as to the status of any of your exhibits, re-offer them before you rest.

Each exhibit has its own standards of authenticity and admissibility. For our purposes, they are better demonstrated than described.

PROBLEM 5

Gun

Part 1 — Actual Gun

Assume that the case is at trial.

(a) For the plaintiff, introduce into evidence the .38 Smith and Wesson gun allegedly used by Lauren Jones in the robbery of Carletti's Market. Prepare an exhibit consistent with the information in the case file. You may use any witness(es) you desire to lay the foundation for the exhibit. Examine the witness(es) to the extent necessary to lay the foundation and then offer the exhibit. Be prepared to discuss your choice of witness(es).

(b) For the defendant, oppose the examination of the witness(es) and the offer of the exhibit. Be prepared to voir dire the witness(es) on the admissibility of the exhibit.

Part 2 — Similar Gun

Assume that the case is at trial.

Assume further that the .38 Smith and Wesson gun was introduced into evidence at the preliminary hearing, but that it was not returned to police custody and now is lost.

(a) For the state, introduce into evidence a gun similar to the one allegedly used by Lauren Jones in the robbery of Carletti's Market. Prepare an exhibit consistent with the information in the case file and this problem. You may use any witness(es) you desire to lay the foundation for its use as demonstrative evidence. Examine the witness(es) to the extent necessary to lay the foundation and then offer the exhibit. Be prepared to discuss your choice of witness(es).

(b) For the defendant, oppose the examination of the witness(es) and the offer of the exhibit. Be prepared to voir dire the witness(es) on the admissibility of the exhibit.

PROBLEM 6

Newspaper

Ted Hoynes maintains the Nita *Morning Globe's* library, which includes copies of all back issues of the newspaper. Assume that Hoynes has been issued a subpoena duces tecum to produce the May 9, YR-0, edition of the Nita Morning Globe with particular reference to the "Today's Sports on Television" section, which is in the case file.

Assume further that Mary Burns and Lawrence Roberts have testified for the defense, and that Hoynes is the defendant's next witness.

(a) For the defendant, introduce into evidence the newspaper clipping through the testimony of Mr. Hoynes.

(b) For the state, oppose the examination of the witness(es) and the offer of the exhibit. Be prepared to voir dire the witness on the admissibility of the exhibit.

PROBLEM 7

Gun Registrations

Assume that the case is at trial.

(a) For the state, introduce into evidence the two gun registrations. You may use any witness(es) you desire to lay the foundation for the exhibits. Examine the witness(es) to the extent necessary to lay the foundation and then offer the exhibits. Be prepared to discuss your choice of witness(es).

(b) For the defendant, oppose the examination of the witness(es) and the offer of the exhibits. Be prepared to voir dire the witness(es) on the admissibility of the exhibits.

USE OF VISUAL AIDS

1. *Visual Aids in General.* In addition to exhibits that are offered and received in evidence on the basis of their intrinsic relevance to the case, visual aids frequently are used by lawyers during examinations of witnesses. These aids are exhibits that assist witnesses in explaining their testimony. Such exhibits, in and of themselves, are not relevant to the case; their relevance flows from the fact that by assisting a witness in testifying, they enhance the probative value of the testimony. The phrase "visual *aid*" as opposed to "demonstrative *evidence*" indicates that the exhibit's evidentiary value is derived from its role in assisting the witness as opposed to any intrinsic evidentiary value.

   The foundation for visual aids is based on the same four touchstones that govern other exhibits: authenticity, relevance, the hearsay rule and the best evidence rule. For authenticity and the hearsay and best evidence rules, the foundation depends on the particular exhibit and will be determined on an individual basis. The general analysis of the necessary foundation, however, is the same as that used for all other exhibits.

   The relevance foundation for visual aids is testimony establishing that the exhibit will assist a witness in explaining his or her testimony. By permitting the court or the jury to more fully understand the value of the testimony of a witness, the exhibit enhances the probative value of the testimony. The countervailing arguments on the question of relevance are that the exhibit raises collateral issues, wastes time, or is unduly prejudicial. In ruling on the use of visual aids, courts employ the classic relevancy balancing test, meaning the use of such aids is discretionary with the court. Most judges are inclined to permit their use as aids to understanding witness testimony if they will not unduly emphasize that testimony.

2. *Diagrams.* In many jurisdictions, diagrams are *sui generis* and may be classified as either demonstrative evidence or visual aids depending on their relevance to the case. If testimony establishes that a diagram is a fair and accurate representation of something that is relevant, then the diagram is demonstrative evidence. The foundation required for diagrams is essentially the same as that required for photographs. (What is the purpose of the offer? Is the exhibit, when used for that purpose, relevant? Does the exhibit fairly and accurately represent what it purports to represent?) If what is depicted by an authentic diagram is not itself relevant to the case, the diagram is not admissible as demonstrative evidence. But if the diagram is authentic and will assist a witness in explaining his or her testimony, then it is helpful to a better understanding of the evidence and, thus, relevant. The diagram is then admissible as a visual aid for use in assisting the witness. In summary, a diagram usually is admissible as demonstrative evidence if it is authentic and in itself relevant to the case, and a diagram is admissible as a or visual aid if it is authentic and will assist a witness in testifying.

In some jurisdictions, however, diagrams are not admissible as demonstrative evidence under any circumstances and may be used in court solely as visual aids. Although a diagram may be authentic (i.e., it is what it purports to be), courts in those jurisdictions do not consider a diagram to be a sufficiently fair and accurate representation of the real thing to permit its admission as demonstrative evidence. Those courts' rationale is that a diagram by nature only depicts a one- dimensional view. Those courts do permit diagrams to be used to assist witnesses in testifying. In other words, they allow diagrams to be used as visual aids but not as demonstrative evidence.

In all jurisdictions, a diagram need not be drawn to scale to be admitted or used at trial. The fact that a diagram is not to scale affects its weight and not its admissibility or use. If the diagram is not being offered or represented as a scale drawing, then the fact-finder can consider and weigh that factor in evaluating the exhibit.

3. *Problems in the Use of Visual Aids.* Problems in the use of demonstrative or visual aids generally occur because of the lawyer's lack of skill in dealing with the device once he or she has been granted permission from the court to use it. One common shortcoming is the lawyer's failure to introduce the witness to the aid prior to the time he or she testifies. It is not sufficient that the witness be familiar with the subject matter illustrated in the aid. Unless the witness has seen the device and has become sufficiently familiar with the particular illustration involved, the testimony can be disastrous.

The trial lawyers also should be careful to preserve the record for appeal. Words such as "right here" and "at this point" will not have meaning to an appellate court. If the witness's testimony is to have any value on appeal, it must be translated in some manner into words or markings.

PROBLEM 8

Chalkboard and Diagram

Assume that the case is at trial.

Part 1 — Chalkboard

(a) For the state, conduct a direct examination of a witness selected at your option using a chalkboard to illustrate the layout of Carletti's Market.

(b) For the defendant, oppose the use of a chalkboard diagram as a demonstrative aid and conduct a cross examination of the witness.

Part 2 — Diagram

(a) For the state, conduct a direct examination of a witness selected at your option using the diagram in the case file to illustrate the layout of Carletti's Market. Prepare a diagram large enough to be seen by the jury.

(b) For the defendant, oppose the use of the diagram as a demonstrative aid and conduct a cross examination of the witness.

PROBLEM 9

Diagram

Assume that the case is at trial.

(a) For the defendant, conduct a direct examination of Mary Burns using the diagram in the case file to illustrate her testimony. Prepare a diagram large enough to be seen by the jury.

(b) For the state, oppose the use of the diagram as a demonstrative aid and conduct a cross examination of Mrs. Burns.

IMPEACHMENT AND REHABILITATION

Impeachment

Although it is a part of the cross examiner's art, impeachment is a sufficiently difficult problem in itself to warrant separate consideration.

1. The cross examiner must consider not only how to impeach, but also whether the witness should be impeached at all. Just as the trial lawyer should not cross examine in some situations, he or she often may decide wisely that, although impeaching evidence is available, it should not be used. If the witness has not hurt your case, usually it is better not to impeach and risk offending the jury. If the testimony of a witness can be turned to your advantage, as in the case of a truly impartial expert witness, do so and do not impeach.

2. Foundation for impeachment by prior inconsistent statement:

    (a) Under the law of most jurisdictions, the witness must be confronted with a prior inconsistent statement during cross examination. If his or her attention has not been called to the earlier statement, extrinsic evidence of it will not be admissible. Cross examination should be specific as to the time, circumstances and content of the earlier statement.

    (b) The rule requiring a foundation for prior inconsistent statements is relaxed under the Federal Rules of Evidence. Federal Rule 613(b) provides that the witness must be "afforded an opportunity to explain or deny" the prior inconsistent statement in order for extrinsic evidence to be admissible, but no time sequence is specified. Therefore, as long as the witness is available to explain the inconsistency if he so desires, extrinsic proof is admissible.

    (c) Most advocates will prefer to lay a foundation on cross examination irrespective of whether or not it is required under the rules. The reason for this is two-fold. First, the witness may admit the statement, making extrinsic evidence unnecessary. More significantly, confronting a witness with his or her own inconsistency often will have a dramatic impact that cannot be duplicated by introducing evidence of the earlier statement through another person.

3. If the witness denies making an earlier statement, be prepared to prove it by extrinsic evidence.

4. If the witness admits making an inconsistent or otherwise impeaching statement, do not ask questions that give him or her an opportunity to explain it away, unless you are certain that that cannot be done. The attorney who has called the witness will have an opportunity on redirect examination to elicit explanations, if any are available. This affords you the opportunity for re-cross.

5. There is no need, and it is usually harmful, to dwell on the impeaching matter after it has been brought out in cross examination. Remember, you have a closing argument.

Rehabilitation

If a witness has been impeached during cross examination, counsel must evaluate whether to attempt to rehabilitate the witness on redirect examination.

1. As with any redirect examination, counsel should limit the scope of the redirect to those items in which the witness needs an opportunity to explain or amplify upon his testimony after the cross examination. Redirect examination and rehabilitation of a witness is not the time to rehash the direct testimony once again.

2. In considering whether to rehabilitate a witness on redirect examination, counsel should first of all be absolutely certain that the witness has, in fact, been impeached. If the witness has not been effectively impeached, do not attempt to rehabilitate the witness as you may only make matters worse.

3. Rehabilitation generally consists of providing the witness with an opportunity to explain the circumstances pertaining to the impeachment and to elicit any "exculpatory" factors. Give the witness the opportunity to put the impeachment in context.

4. If the impeachment can be explained, do it; if not, leave it alone on redirect as you just may make matters worse.

5. If the witness has been impeached by a prior inconsistent statement, counsel should consider the admissibility of any prior consistent statements. See 801(d)(1)(B) of the Federal Rules of Evidence. Prior consistent statements are generally admissible if they rebut an express or implied charge of recent fabrication.

PROBLEM 10

Lauren Jones

Assume that the case is at trial and Lauren Jones is the first witness for the state. Assume further that Jones has testified on direct examination consistent with the statement that he gave to the police on May 12, YR-1.

(a) For the defense, conduct a cross examination and impeachment of Mr. Jones.

(b) For the state, conduct a redirect examination to the extent it is necessary to rehabilitate the witness.

PROBLEM 11

Mary Burns

Assume that Mary Burns was called as a defense witness. During the course of her testimony she stated that she called the police to report the gun missing on May 1, YR-1, but that the officer who answered the phone told her he was too busy to take the call at that time. In addition, she testified on direct examination that she heard Larry Roberts drive up and park in the driveway and saw his familiar penny loafers walk by the basement window.

(a) For the state, conduct a cross examination and impeachment of Mrs. Burns on these points.

(b) For the defendant, conduct a redirect examination to the extent it is necessary to rehabilitate the witness.

PROBLEM 12

John Burns

Assume that the case is at trial and that John Burns has testified on direct examination as follows:

> After the phone call, my wife went downstairs to do the laundry. She was in and out of the living room several times while I was watching the Red Sox-Yankees game on television. I never left the house between 3:30 and 4:30.

Assume further that the rest of Burn's direct testimony followed his statement in the case file.

(a) For the state, conduct a cross examination and impeachment of Mr. Burns.

(b) For the defendant, conduct a redirect examination to the extent it is necessary to rehabilitate the witness.

ADVERSE EXAMINATION

Adverse examination is the examination of an opposing party or a witness that is specified as being adverse under the applicable evidence rules. Under the Federal Rules of Evidence, a witness who is "identified with the opposing party" is considered to be an adverse witness. *See* FRE 611(c) and the Advisory Committee's Notes.

In form, the party calling the witness, the adverse examiner, conducts a direct examination, and the opponent conducts a cross examination. In substance, however, the direct examination of the adverse witness involves the interrogation of an unwilling, biased, and unsympathetic witness, who has not been prepared by the party who has called the witness. The circumstances are the same as in cross examination and, therefore, leading questions are permitted.

After the adverse examination, the party opponent has an opportunity to cross examine the adverse witness. The form of the examination is that of cross examination, but that is typically not the substance of the interrogation. In other than multi-party cases, the witness is the cross examiner's client or a witness identified with the client. The witness has been prepared by the cross examiner and is certainly not unwilling, biased, or hostile. Essentially this is the same as a direct examination and leading questions usually will not be permitted. *See* FRE 611(c).

Different considerations may be involved in multi-party cases. It may be necessary to analyze each issue in the case to determine if there is adversity. Parties defendant may be adverse to each other on some issues and have a community of interest on others. Leading questions are appropriate only when there are adverse interests.

By calling an adverse witness, the examining party has the opportunity to determine the scope of the examination and thus to pick and choose what subjects are to be raised. Under the rules of most jurisdictions, including the federal rules, the cross examiner is limited to the scope of the adverse examination as determined by the examining party. Thus, the cross examination of an adverse witness is limited to the subjects brought out during the adverse examination.

Adverse examination, in the opinion of many trial lawyers, is the ultimate weapon. It is ultimate in the sense that it should be used rarely and then only with the greatest of care and control.

When it is employed it usually is for a very limited purpose, for example, to authenticate a document that is essential to the examiner's case. But there are occasions in which the trial lawyer will believe that tactics require a full, searching, in-court adverse examination.

Often lawyers will disagree on whether a particular situation is a proper setting for an adverse examination. There are at least two common bases for this disagreement. First, while the adverse examiner is not "bound" by the witness's testimony and may impeach the witness, the examiner nevertheless is eliciting the testimony during his or her case. Thus, if the adverse witness makes a good impression on the fact-finder, and his or her testimony is not helpful (or, worse, is harmful) to the examiner's case, the psychological effect on the fact-finder can be devastating to the examiner's case. The countervailing point is that the examining lawyer should be thoroughly prepared by depositions or investigation. The witness can and should be controlled by leading questions if there has been proper preparation.

Secondly, in many cases, selected portions of the adverse witness' deposition testimony are admissible on the offer of the examiner as admissions by a party opponent. This is a safer route to take and lawyers, being a cautious lot, frequently will opt for the safe route. The counterargument is that reading a deposition is a dry exercise, totally devoid of demeanor and not very persuasive. By using the deposition to control the live witness, however, counsel can make a point through the witness' own mouth, on the stand and under oath.

Despite these caveats about the use of the ultimate weapon, developing the skill of its use is mandatory. Here are some basic guidelines:

1. Frame your questions with great care. No "open" questions can be risked here. You may lead and you should do so.

2. Control the witness. Do not permit the witness to avoid the question. The witness must not be permitted to ramble or volunteer. Remember, you are entitled to responsive answers. Insist on them.

3. Never ask a question to which you do not know the answer and with which you cannot impeach the witness if he answers contrary to your expectation. Here, more than on cross examination, you will "get it" if you "ask for it."

4. Watch your attitude and demeanor toward the witness. Hostility toward any witness at any time is almost always counterproductive. Here, as on cross examination, there is a tendency to be hostile. You must guard against it. You have called the witness. If the fact-finder senses that you have done so for the purpose of humiliating the witness, it will be held against you.

5. When your adverse examination is concluded, be certain to limit your opponent's examination to those subjects you have covered. Do not permit your opponent to turn your effort into his or her own case.

PROBLEM 13

Larry Roberts

Although the concept of the adverse witness is largely confined to civil cases, similar problems may arise in the context of a criminal case. Assume that the defense in the *Burns* case did not call Larry Roberts. Instead, he is called as a rebuttal witness for the state.

(a) For the state, conduct an adverse examination of Mr. Roberts on whatever topics you think appropriate. Be ready to discuss: (1) any limitations you put on the scope of your examination; (2) the order of witnesses in which you called Mr. Roberts; and (3) whether, in an actual trial, you would have called Mr. Roberts.

(b) For the defendant, conduct a cross examination of Mr. Roberts.

(c) For the state, conduct any necessary re-adverse examination.

PROBLEM 14

Mary Burns

Assume that the case is at trial and the state has called Mary Burns, the wife of the defendant, as an adverse witness. Assume further that Mrs. Burns has no spousal privilege against testifying and is not an incompetent witness.

(a) For the state, conduct an adverse examination of Mrs. Burns on whatever topics you think appropriate. Be ready to discuss: (1) any limitations you put on the scope of your examination; (2) the order of witnesses in which you called Mrs. Burns; and (3) whether, in an actual trial, you would have called Mrs. Burns.

(b) For the defendant, conduct a cross examination of Mrs. Burns.

(c) For the state, conduct any necessary re-adverse examination.

WITNESS PREPARATION

Chronologically, this topic should precede all that has gone before. As other teachers of trial advocacy have observed, however, exposure to the pitfalls of the courtroom sharpens the trial lawyer's awareness of the need for thorough witness preparation. (See, for example, the sequence of exercises in A. Levin and H. Cramer, *Trial Advocacy, Problems and Materials,* Foundation Press, 1968.) Hopefully, that has been the case here.

From a coaching standpoint, this topic might well be eliminated. In the privacy of a lawyer's office, there are no rules of evidence to restrain the preparation and examination of witnesses. Further, when one multiplies the lawyer types by the myriad of witness types, the number of combinations is infinite. Thus, it is impossible to actually teach witness preparation.

A great deal has been written on the subject. There are a variety of common sense admonitions calculated to put a witness in the most favorable and persuasive posture: be at ease; don't chew gum on the stand; dress neatly and conservatively; listen to the question and don't answer it until it is completed; don't worry about where counsel is going on direct or cross examination; just answer the questions.

There are, however, some questions about witness preparation and some problems which recur with remarkable frequency that should be raised. The following problems are intended to illustrate them. As you confront them, keep in mind that our English brothers at the bar seldom encounter them, for in England it is regarded as unethical for the barrister to "wood-shed" the witness.

PROBLEM 15

Lauren Jones

You have interviewed Lauren Jones in detail and have talked with him about this case on several occasions. Each time he has answered questions in a manner consistent with his second statement and preliminary hearing testimony. It is the day before the trial.

Interview Mr. Jones and prepare him for trial.

PROBLEM 16

John Burns

Assume for the purposes of this problem that John Burns is currently free on $20,000 bail. He and his wife put up their residence as security for this bond. The case is set for trial in two weeks. Assume further that Burns has told you he has a witness he wants you to call during his case.

Interview Mr. Burns and prepare him for trial.

PROBLEM 17

Arthur Hellman

Assume that as the assistant attorney general handling this case you have read the police reports prepared by Detective Arthur Hellman and have reviewed Hellman's testimony at the preliminary hearing. This will be your first meeting with Hellman. It is three weeks before trial.

Interview Detective Hellman and prepare him for trial.

ADVANCED DIRECT AND CROSS EXAMINATION

The Defendant in a Criminal Case

The question of a defendant testifying at trial raises difficult problems for the criminal defense lawyer. The most critical decision is whether to call the client at all. In Problem 180 consider not only the direct and cross examination possibilities but also whether the defendant should testify and, if so, at what point during the trial he should be called.

PROBLEM 18

John Burns

Assume that the state has presented its case and that the defendant's motion for nonsuit has been denied. The defense calls John Burns as its first witness. For purposes of this problem, the examinations should be limited to the matter of Burns' alleged alibi.

(a) For the defendant, conduct a direct examination of Mr. Burns.

(b) For the state, conduct a cross examination of Mr. Burns.

(c) For the defendant, conduct any necessary redirect examination.

PROBLEM 19

Lauren Jones

Assume that the state has begun presentation of its case in chief and James Carletti has testified. The state calls Lauren Jones as its next witness.

(a) For the state, conduct a direct examination of Mr. Jones.

(b) For the defendant, conduct a cross examination of Mr. Jones.

(c) For the state, conduct any necessary redirect examination.

PROBLEM 20

James Carletti

Assume that the case is at trial and the state has called James Carletti as its first witness. Assume further that Carletti is extremely bitter, believing that the defendant, as the mastermind of the attempted robbery, is responsible for his wife's death.

(a) For the state, conduct a direct examination of Mr. Carletti.

(b) For the defendant, conduct a cross examination of Mr. Carletti.

(c) For the state, conduct any necessary redirect examination.

JURY SELECTION

If one were to interview ten able trial lawyers at random with regard to how to select a jury, one would get ten different answers. The answers would range from, "Take the first twelve (or six) and put them in the box," to "Examine each juror firmly and searchingly." We will discuss the pros and cons of both attitudes as well as the way stations between.

There is virtual unanimity among trial lawyers that the makeup of the jury is important. There is also agreement among those who watch trial lawyers at work that we do a pretty fair job of jury selection, regardless of how we do it or why we excuse those who are excused.

There are certain basic guidelines that should be followed in selecting a jury:

1. In those jurisdictions that permit the lawyers to interrogate the veniremen, realize that this is your first direct contact with the jurors. Don't alienate them. Don't try them.

2. Know the statutory qualifications for jurors and the case law grounds for the challenge for cause.

3. Know the number of peremptories to which you are entitled.

4. Never challenge a juror for cause in the presence of that juror unless you have a peremptory by which you can excuse him if your challenge is overruled.

5. Use your peremptories wisely. Do not spend them too quickly.

6. Be alert for jurors whose background and experience indicate that they possess knowledge particularly relevant to the facts in the case. You may end up with a one-juror jury.

7. Be alert for jurors whose background and experience indicate a high potential of prejudgment of the case adverse to your position. They may hang the jury.

8. Seek a cross-section of the community, but bear in mind that studies have indicated a correlation between ethnic-socio-economic background and juror vote.

PROBLEM 21

Jury Selection in State v. Burns

Select a jury for one of the parties in the case. To permit an in-depth interrogation and analysis of each juror within a limited time frame, only four jurors will be selected. Each side will be limited to one peremptory challenge. Use the following jury information sheet.

Jury Information Sheet

Please assume the role of a person whom you know well, so you will be able to answer *voir dire* questions in that role. Please be realistic. Try to pick a role that will be commonly represented on jury panels *and not a role of an eccentric.* Your taking an eccentric role would seriously impair the realism and benefit of the exercise for your classmates, both those who serve as counsel and those who observe the exercise.

Please fill in the following form and be prepared to use it at the class session on Jury Selection. You may be asked to deliver it to the instructor in advance of the class or during the class session.

Your real name: ______________________________

Information About You in Your Assumed Role

1. Name: ______________________________
2. Age: ______________________________
3. Address in Nita City: ______________________________

   Characterize the neighborhood: ______________________________
4. Length of residence in Nita City: ______________________________
5. Occupation: ______________________________

   Duties in that occupation: ______________________________
6. Marital status: ______________________________
7. Number and ages of children: ______________________________
8. Number of years of education: ______________________________
9. Other relevant information: ______________________________

OPENING STATEMENT

The opening statement is akin to the first scene in a play — it had better capture the audience. It is the trial lawyer's first direct contact with the jury, save in those jurisdictions that permit substantial lawyer participation in the voir dire examination of the jury. Even in those states, in the overwhelming majority of cases, it is the lawyer's first opportunity to present the jury with an intelligent, cohesive description of the case.

Some trial lawyers tend to minimize the importance of an opening statement. We do no. We regard it as crucial to the successful outcome of the trial.

There is no excuse for a poor opening statement (unless, of course, the case is so poor it should not be tried). The opening statement is essentially *ex parte*; it can and should be prepared well in advance of its presentation, and it should be rehearsed.

It is a skill that can be mastered with practice more readily than any other skill. The general guidelines for opening statements are:

1. Practice, rehearse, try out, and listen to your opening statements before you make them. You have a wife, a husband, a friend, a colleague who will listen if you ask. As you rehearse, you can listen, too. The preferred audience is a lay one.

2. Recognize the opening for what it is: a prologue or synopsis of a play, a blueprint, a travel guide folder, or the old favorite — the picture on the jigsaw puzzle box. We do not urge that you use these similes when you address the jury. We do urge that you recognize the opening statement for what it is. Indeed, in conjunction with the evidentiary portion of the trial and the closing argument, it is the trial lawyer's application of the oldest of public speaking techniques: tell your audience what you are going to say, say it, and tell them what you have said.

3. Recognize the opening statement for what it is not: it is not an argument. This is not the time to infer, plead, or fulminate. It is a time to tell the jury what the case is about and what you expect your evidence will be.

4. An opening statement in behalf of the plaintiff or prosecution should include:

    (a) A request of the court and the jury: "If the court please, ladies and gentlemen of the jury."

    (b) An introduction of yourself, your client, your opponent, and his client, if not already done sufficiently during jury selection.

    (c) A cohesive, succinct, and confident summary of what your evidence will be.

    (d) A conclusion, indicating that at the close of the case you will return and request the jury to find in favor of your client.

(e) Some lawyers include the following either at the beginning or the end of the opening statement:

(i) A brief statement of the nature of the case.

(ii) A brief statement of the issues of the case.

(iii) A candid acknowledgment that the burden of persuasion rests on you and the degree of the burden.

(iv) A reading of the indictment or information (which is required in some jurisdictions).

5. An opening statement in behalf of the plaintiff or prosecution should *not* include:

(a) Reference to evidence, or which the availability or admissibility is doubtful.

(b) Anticipated defenses or defense evidence.

6. In most cases, an opening statement for a defendant should bed made immediately following that of plaintiff or prosecution. If the court has granted you permission to defer your opening statement until the close of your opponent's case, be certain the jury knows this. Be very cautious about waiving a defendant's opening statement entirely.

7. An opening statement in behalf of a defendant should include:

(a) A request of the court and the jury: "If the court please, ladies and gentlemen of the jury."

(b) An introduction (or reintroduction) of yourself and your client, if not already done sufficiently during jury selection.

(c) An admonition that opening statements are not evidence.

(d) An acceptance of the issues as defined by your opponent, plus any additional ones that will be raised by the defense.

(e) A reinforcement of the principle that the burden of persuasion rests with your opponent, plus a candid recognition of any issues in respect to which it rests with you.

(f) A cohesive, succinct, and confident (but non-argumentative) reference to anticipated deficiencies in your opponent's evidence, plus a like summary of what your evidence will be.

(g) A conclusion, indicating that at the close of the case you will return and request the jury to find in favor of your client.

8. As with your counterpart, a defense counsel's opening statement should not include references to evidence of which the availability or admissibility is doubtful.

9. Opening statements for defendant's in criminal cases often present special problems:

   (a) Never assume the burden of proving innocence.

   (b) If you have any doubt as to whether your client will testify, do not tell the jury he will. On the other hand, if you are certain he will testify, tell the jury and admonish it that it cannot fairly form any judgment in the case until it has heard from the defendant.

   (c) We would not presume to outline an opening statement in a "no defense" criminal case. Perhaps we will see one during our exercises.

10. In criminal cases, some jurisdictions permit counsel for the defendant to reserve opening statement until the close of the state's case-in-chief. Counsel should always consider very carefully the pros and cons of reserving the opening statement until after the state's case.

PROBLEM 22

Opening Statements in State v. Burns

Present an opening statement for one of the parties in the case.

If you are preparing an opening statement for a defendant in a criminal case, consider whether you would introduce any evidence for the defendant and whether the defendant is likely to testify. Your opening statement should be planned accordingly.

CLOSING ARGUMENT

Here is the advocate in his final and finest hour! She won it with her closing argument! She was magnificent! Legion are the legends of summations.

A lawsuit is won during the trial, not at the conclusion of it. It is won by the witnesses and the exhibits and the manner in which the lawyer paces, spaces, and handles them.

The likelihood of a lawyer's snatching victory from the jaws of defeat with his or her closing argument is so slight that it hardly warrants consideration. (Compare last of the ninth multi-run, game-winning home runs; *but see* Bobby Thompson's shot heard round the world in *Giants v. Dodgers* (1951).)

On the other hand, lawsuits are lost by fumbling, stumbling, incoherent, exaggerated, vindictive closing arguments.

This is not intended to minimize the importance of the closing argument. It is merely to relegate it to its proper position, which is a summation of the evidence that has preceded it, and a relation of that evidence to the issues in the case.

Although the closing argument is not quite as controllable as is the opening statement, it is very close to it — close enough that we can say that there is no excuse for a poor closing argument.

Many trial lawyers begin to prepare their closing arguments with their first contact with the case: as the facts make their initial impressions on their minds. That is when they are as close to being jurors as they ever will be. From that first impression forward they shape and reshape their closing arguments as the facts develop. Finally they shape the trial to what they believe their strongest arguments will be; they prove their arguments.

Thus, the closing argument has a considerable impact on the trial because an able trial lawyer knows that an argument without evidence to support it is no evidence at all.

The basic guidelines for closing arguments are:

1. Think about, prepare, and rehearse your closing argument before trial, leaving sufficient flexibility to meet the exigencies of trial.

2. Think about, modify, and rehearse your closing argument at each break in the trial in light of the record to date.

3. Think about, modify, and, if time permits, rehearse your closing argument at the close of the evidence and the conference on instructions.

4. Base your closing argument on the issues, the evidence, the burden of proof in the case, and your client's right to a verdict.

5. From the standpoint of format,

   (a) Address the court, the jury, and your opponent.

   (b) Tell the jury your purpose — to summarize the facts and relate them to the issues in the case.

   (c) Make your argument.

   (d) Tell the jury what its verdict should be.

   (e) Sit down.

6. From the standpoint of delivery: do not shout, do not engage in personalities, do not tell the jury what you believe, but act and speak as though you do believe, to the depths of your soul, every word you are uttering. If you can't do the latter, don't argue.

7. As for some of the canned approaches:

   (a) Do no repeat in chronological order the testimony of each witness. Give the jury some credit; it has heard the witnesses. Put it all together.

   (b) Do not tell the jury what you say is not evidence. Why belittle your argument? The judge will do that for you.

   (c) Do not assume a burden of persuasion that is not yours.

PROBLEM 23

Closing Arguments in State v. Burns

Present a closing argument for one of the parties in the case.

In planning your closing, you may assume that you would have offered any or all of the admissible evidence available to your side at the trial. If you are representing the defendant in a criminal case, you should decide whether you would have had the defendant testify or whether you would have offered any evidence at all.

Assume that all of the admissible evidence available to the other party has been offered.

In many jurisdictions, counsel for the party with the burden of proof has the right to give the first closing argument and then a rebuttal argument to the defendant's closing. For the purposes of this problem, counsel for the party with the burden of proof should assume that their closing argument is the first closing argument.

Section II

Case File

STATE v. BURNS

TABLE OF CONTENTS

Page

Introduction 1
Special Instructions for Use as a Full Trial 3
Stipulations 5
Indictment 7
Arrest Warrant 9
Police Report/May 9th/Det. Arthur Hellman 11
Police Report/May 11th/Det. Arthur Hellman 15

Statements for the Prosecution
- James Carletti 17
- Lauren Jones/May 9th 19
- Lauren Jones/May 11th 21

Preliminary Hearing Testimony/May 9th
- James Carletti 23
- Lauren Jones 28
- Detective Arthur Hellman 32

Exhibits
- Newspaper Articles 37
- Diagrams 43
- Arrest Warrants 49
- Motor Vehicle Registration Record 53
- Weapons Registration Records 57
- Death Certificate 63

Statements for the Defense
- John Burns 65
- Memorandum to Defense Counsel 69
- Mary Burns 71
- Laurence Roberts 75

Statutes 77
Case Law 79
Proposed Jury Instructions 81
General Jury Instructions 83
Form of Verdict 89

INTRODUCTION

The Grand Jury has charged John Burns with first degree murder and robbery for the death of Teresa Carletti and the attempted robbery of the Carletti grocery store on May 9, YR-0, in Nita City, Nita.

Lauren Jones was attempting to rob the Carletti grocery store when the owner, James Carletti, pulled a gun from under the counter and fired at Mr. Jones. The bullet missed Jones and struck and killed Carletti's wife, Teresa. Jones was arrested at the scene of the robbery and has pleaded guilty to robbery. No murder charges are pending against him.

The State alleges that the defendant, John Burns, planned the robbery of the grocery store and waited outside in the getaway car while Jones went inside to rob the store. The defendant has been charged with armed robbery for his alleged participation in the holdup and with felony-murder for the death of Mrs. Carletti.

The applicable law is contained in the statutes, case law, and proposed jury instructions that are set forth at the end of the case file.

All years in these materials are stated in the following form:

* YR-0 indicates the actual year in which the case is being tried (i.e., the present year);
* YR-1 indicates the next preceding year (please use the actual year);
* YR-2 indicates the second preceding year (please use the actual year), etc.

Authors' Note: The crime charged occurred in May, YR-0 [current year] and if the case file is used before **June 1** in any given year, please backdate the dating system by one year. For example, YR-0 becomes YR-1; YR-1 becomes YR-2; YR-2 becomes the YR-3; etc.

SPECIAL INSTRUCTIONS FOR USE AS A FULL TRIAL

When this case file is used as the basis for a full trial, the following witnesses may be called by the parties:

For the State:

Arthur Hellman
James Carletti
Lauren Jones

For the Defendant:

John Burns
Mary Burns
Laurence Roberts

A party need not call all of the persons listed as its witnesses. Any or all of the witnesses can be called by either party with the exception that the State cannot call the defendant. However, if a witness is to be called by a party other than the one for whom he or she is listed, the party for whom the witness is listed will select and prepare the witness.

STIPULATIONS

Assume that in the State of Nita a defendant has the right to request a preliminary hearing in all felony cases. Thus, a defendant in a criminal case involving a felony charge has the right to a preliminary hearing regardless of whether the criminal prosecution was initiated by either an indictment or an information.

The parties have agreed to the following stipulations:

1. All of the documents and newspaper clippings in the case file are authentic.

2. The Smith and Wesson .38 referred to in the case file is authentic.

3. The defendant has waived his rights under the Nita Speedy Trial Statute.

4. The date, May 9, YR-0, on which the robbery occurred and Mrs. Carletti was killed was a Saturday.

5. The date, May 10, YR-0, was a Sunday and it was Mother's Day.

6. The Nita Motor Vehicle Code requires that automobiles display front and rear license plates.

IN THE SUPERIOR COURT OF
DARROW COUNTY
STATE OF NITA

THE PEOPLE OF THE STATE OF NITA vs. JOHN BURNS Defendant.	)))))))	Case No. CR 324 INDICTMENT

The Grand Jury, in and for the County of Darrow, State of Nita, upon their oath and in the name and by the authority of the State of Nita, does hereby charge the following offenses under the Criminal Code of the State of Nita:

Count I

That on May 9, YR-0, at and within the County of Darrow in the State of Nita, John Burns committed the crime of

ARMED ROBBERY

in violation of Section 18-6-302 of the Nita Criminal Code of 1974, as amended, in that he, together with another participant, Lauren Jones, did take a thing of value, United States currency, from the person and presence of James S. Carletti by the use of threats, force, and intimidation by displaying a deadly weapon, a gun.

Contrary to the form of the Statute and against the peace and dignity of the People of the State of Nita.

Count II

That on May 9, YR-0, at and within the County of Darrow in the State of Nita, John Burns committed the crime of

MURDER IN THE FIRST DEGREE

in violation of Section 18-3-102(1)(b) of the Nita Criminal Code of 1974, as amended, in that he, together with another participant, Lauren Jones, did attempt to and did commit the crime of Robbery, and in the course of and in furtherance of committing that crime, the death of a person not a participant, Teresa Carletti, was caused by a bullet fired from a gun by the victim of that Robbery, James S. Carletti.

Contrary to the form of the Statute and against the peace and dignity of the People of the State of Nita.

This the 20th day of May, YR-0.

A TRUE BILL:

Anthony Alifano
District Attorney

Bernadette Brown
Foreperson of the Grand Jury

STATE OF NITA
County of Darrow

File # ______
Film # ______

In The General Court of Justice
District Court Division

The State of Nita vs.

John Burns
Defendant

WARRANT FOR ARREST

Age	Race	Sex	Occupation
35		M	

221 Elm St., Nita City, Nita
Address

To any officer with authority and territorial jurisdiction to execute a warrant for arrest for the offense charged below:

THE UNDERSIGNED FINDS THAT THERE IS PROBABLE CAUSE TO BELIEVE that on or about the 9th day of May, YR-0, in the county named above, the defendant named above, acting with Lauren Jones, committed a robbery of Carletti's IGA Market at 401 Main St., Nita City, Nita, and in the course of the robbery, one Teresa Carletti was killed.

in violation of the following law: G.S.18-3-102(1)(b) and 18-6-302.

YOU ARE DIRECTED TO ARREST THE DEFENDANT NAMED ABOVE AND BRING HIM WITHOUT UNNECESSARY DELAY BEFORE A JUDICIAL OFFICIAL TO ANSWER THE CHARGES SET OUT ABOVE.

Issued this 11th day of May, YR-0, upon information furnished under oath by the complainant or complainants named below.

Complainant(s) Name, Address or Department

James S. Carletti
Arthur Hellman

Jonathan J. Taylor
Magistrate

NITA CITY POLICE DEPARTMENT
NITA CITY, NITA

ARREST REPORT

1 ARREST NUMBER 3182-YR-0	2 PRINTS [X] PHOTOS [X]	3 NAME LAST / FIRST / MIDDLE Jones / Lauren / NMI		
4 ALIAS/NICKNAME Spike	5 DATE OF BIRTH 7/31/YR-28	6 AGE 28	7 SEX M	8 RACE/ETHNIC C
9 ADDRESS 3300 Hillgrand Drive, Nita City, Nita	PHONE unkwn	10 PLACE OF BIRTH Meriden, Nita		
11 HEIGHT 5' 10"	12 WEIGHT 160	13 HAIR Brown	14 EYES Brown	15 COMPLEXION Fair/clear
16 SOC. SEC. NUMBER 049-36-4748				
17 OPERATOR LICENSE NUMBER & STATE N-5182564	18 MISCELLANEOUS	19 OCCUPATION unemployed		
20 EMPLOYEE/SCHOOL N/A	21 ADDRESS N/A	PHONE unknown		

DETAILS OF ARREST

22 DATE OF ARREST (MO DAY YR) 5/9/YR-0	23 TIME (24 hr clock) 1620	24 HOW ARRESTED ON VIEW [X] WARRANT [ ] ORDER FOR ARREST [ ]		
25 PLACE OF ARREST 401 Main Street, Nita City, Nita (Carletti's IGA)				
26 INITIAL CHARGE Murder	27 COUNTS 1	28 STATUTE 18-6-102 (1)(b)	29 OFFENSE JURISDICTION Nita City & Darrow County	30 WARRANT DATE (MO DAY YR) N/A
31 SUBSEQUENT CHARGE Armed robbery	32 COUNTS 1	33 STATUTE 18-6-302	34 OFFENSE JURISDICTION Nita City & Darrow County	35 WARRANT DATE (MO DAY YR) N/A
36 VEHICLE INFORMATION LICENSE # N/A STATE N/A MAKE N/A VIN N/A	37 PLACE STORED N/A			
38 VEHICLE INVENTORY INFORMATION (MO DAY YR) BY: N/A				
39 COMPLAINANT'S NAME James Silvio Carletti	ADDRESS 61 Hill Avenue, Nita City, Nita	PHONE unknown		

CONFINEMENT/BOND INFORMATION

40 DATE CONFINED (MO DAY YR) 5/ 9/YR-0	TIME (24 Hour Clock) 1650	41 PLACE CONFINED Nita City Jail	42 COMMITTING MAGISTRATE Gregory S. Lewis
43 TYPE BOND None	44 AMOUNT N/A	45 DATE RELEASED (MO DAY YR) / TIME (24 HOUR CLOCK)	46 RELEASED BY N/A

DISPOSITION INFORMATION

47 DEPOSITION DATE (MO DAY YR) 5/18/YR-0	48 COURT DOCKET YR-0-6969	49 COURT/JUDGE / CITY Darrow County-Superior Court in Nita City
50 DISPOSITION Plea. guilty robbery/murder dismissed with leave	51 SENTENCE Continued at request of District Attorney	

52 NARRATIVE On 5/9/YR-0 I was summoned to Carletti's IGA Market at 401 Main St., Nita City, Nita, where there had been a reported attempted robbery and shooting. I received the call at approximately 4:15 p.m. and proceeded directly to the scene of the offense. Upon arrival, I found the owner of the market, James S. Carletti, who was holding at gun point the defendant, Lauren Jones. I also discovered the owner's wife, Teresa B. Carletti lying in a pool of blood adjacent to the magazine rack along the

RIGHT THUMB

53 ARRESTING OFFICER -- NAME AND SIGNATURE Det. Arthur Hellman, NCPD	54 DATE/SUBMITTED (MO DAY YR) 5/12/YR-0	TIME (24 Hour Clock) 300
55 SUPERVISOR SIGNATURE J. McCormick	56 ARRESTEE SIGNATURE	

NITA CITY POLICE DEPARTMENT
NITA CITY, NITA
ARREST REPORT—CONTINUATION PAGE

1 ARREST NUMBER	2 NAME LAST / FIRST / MIDDLE	3 ALIAS/NICKNAME
3182-YR-0	Jones Lauren NMI	Spike

4 COMPLAINANT'S NAME	ADDRESS	PHONE
James Silvio Carletti	61 Hill Avenue, Nita City, Nita	unknown

5 NARRATIVE

front window of the store. Mrs. Carletti was apparently dead. An ambulance had already been summoned. I placed the defendant, Lauren Jones, under arrest for robbery and murder and obtained a statement from the owner, Mr. Carletti. He was in a very disturbed state but I was able to ascertain the following facts. On 5/9/YR-0, the defendant, Lauren Jones, entered the above described premises at approximately 4:00 p.m. His face was covered with a blue and white bandana. He was pointing a pistol at Mr. Carletti and demanded all the money from the register. Jones got impatient and pushed the cash button on the register. At that point, Mr. Carletti reached under the cash register counter and withdrew a .22 caliber pistol and rapidly fired one shot. Jones had ducked underneath the counter and the shot struck Mrs. Carletti. Jones yelled out that his weapon was not loaded and not to shoot. Mr. Carletti then proceeded to where his wife had fallen and talked to her briefly before she died. I was unable to ascertain the contents of their conversation before Mr. Carletti broke down completely. Defendant Jones was taken to police headquarters by Officer Yank of N.C.P.D. I took into custody both the Carletti .22 pistol and the weapon found in the possession of the defendant. The defendant's weapon was a .38 caliber Smith & Wesson pistol. I ascertained that the firing pin had been removed from that weapon. Both weapons were placed in evidence bags which I kept in my possession until I returned to the station house whereupon they were inventoried and secured in the N.C.P.D. evidence locker. Serial Nos. on the two weapons are as follows: .22 caliber pistol 348X75H498; .38 caliber Smith & Wesson pistol V672952. I then drove Mr. Carletti to the home of his neighbor, Walter Dellinger. At that point, Mr. Carletti had calmed down some and I asked if he could give me a more compete statement concerning the events in question. He consented to do so and gave me a signed statement that I typed out on Mr. Dellinger's typewriter that was witnessed by Mr. Dellinger and myself. Later at the police station, I informed Mr. Jones again of his Miranda rights. I asked him if he understood his rights and he responded in the affirmative. I then talked to him and he gave a statement to the police stenographer which he later signed with a notary present.

5/10/YR-0—Continued investigation in the above matter. Signed out .38 caliber Smith & Wesson pistol from the evidence locker for the purpose of performing fingerprint analysis. Analysis indicated a complete set of prints from the defendant Lauren Jones on the gun butt and trigger. There was also one unidentified latent thumb print on top of the gun barrel just forward of the firing mechanism. The print was positioned so that the fingernail would have been pointing towards the hammer and the rest of the finger towards the muzzle. Returned above-described pistol to the evidence locker and signed it

6 OFFICER'S NAME	7 OFFICER'S SIGNATURE
Det. Arthur Hellman	Det. Arthur Hellman

8 DATE/SUBMITTED MO DAY YR	TIME 24 Hour Clock	9 SUPERVISOR'S NAME	10
5/13/YR-0		J. McCormick	Page 2 of 4

NITA CITY POLICE DEPARTMENT
NITA CITY, NITA
ARREST REPORT—CONTINUATION PAGE

1 ARREST NUMBER	2 NAME LAST / FIRST / MIDDLE	3 ALIAS/NICKNAME
3182-YR-0	Jones Lauren NMI	Spike

4 COMPLAINANT'S NAME	ADDRESS	PHONE
James Silvio Carletti	61 Hill Avenue, Nita City, Nita	unknown

5 NARRATIVE

back in. I once again spoke to the defendant Jones with his consent and he informed me that he had nothing further to say about the matter.

5/11/YR-0—Continued investigation in above matter. Jones was arraigned at 9:00 a.m. on Murder and Robbery charges. With Mr. Carletti's permission, I gained entrance into the premises at 401 Main Street and took various measurements and made a to-scale diagram of the market area in question. Called in serial numbers of the two weapons in question to Nita Weapon Registration Department to ascertain whether the weapons were registered. Ascertained that .22 caliber pistol, serial no. 348X75H498, was registered to James Silvio Carletti of 61 Hill Avenue, Nita City, Nita, and that .38 caliber Smith & Wesson pistol, serial no. V672952, was registered to Mary N. Burns of 221 Elm Street, Nita City, Nita. Checked with larceny division to see if that weapon had been reported stolen and found that the theft of the weapon had been reported by the owner at 9:00 a.m. that morning. Checked with motor vehicles to ascertain what type of car, if any, was registered to Mary N. Burns at the above address. Motor vehicles reported that a YR-1, 2-door, green, Oldsmobile Cutlass was registered to John Burns at the same address, 221 Elm St., Nita City, Nita. Requested that D.M.V. send confirmation of that registration to me at N.C.P.D. Then called the Nita Weapon Registration Department and asked that they send confirmation of the weapon registration to Mary Burns noted above to N.C.P.D. Checked with N.C.P.D. records to ascertain if we had any records of John Burns and found that he had two convictions for possession of heroin and had been arrested on numerous occasions in the past five years, but that no convictions had resulted. All arrests were for gambling related offenses, so spoke to head of Vice Squad for N.C.P.D. for further information. Was informed by Lieutenant Davison that Burns was a suspected numbers runner and more recently a higher up in local organized crime. Davison informed me that if we could get a conviction on Burns that it as likely that he would inform on the leadership in Darrow County organized crime. Then pulled records on Burns, along with fingerprints on file. Compared latent thumb print, previously unidentified on .38 caliber Smith & Wesson pistol taken from Defendant Jones. Comparison was positive. Left thumb print on pistol matched left thumb print in Burns's file. Then proceeded to talk to Jones. Informed Jones that I had a lead on the driver of the vehicle that delivered him to the front of Carletti's Market and asked if he would like to cooperate. He asked what was in it for him so I told him that I'd have to talk it over with the District Attorney. Spoke to the District Attorney on the phone. He informed me that he concurred in Lt. Davison's analysis of the Burns situation and informed me that in return for truthful information from Jones

6 OFFICER'S NAME	7 OFFICER'S SIGNATURE
Det. Arthur Hellman	Det. Arthur Hellman

8 DATE/SUBMITTED MO DAY YR	TIME 24 Hour Clock	9 SUPERVISOR'S NAME	10
5/12/YR-0	300	J. McCormick	Page 3 of 4

NITA CITY POLICE DEPARTMENT
NITA CITY, NITA

ARREST REPORT—CONTINUATION PAGE

1 ARREST NUMBER	2 NAME LAST / FIRST / MIDDLE	3 ALIAS/NICKNAME
3182-YR-0	Jones Lauren NMI	Spike

4 COMPLAINANT'S NAME	ADDRESS	PHONE
James Silvio Carletti	61 Hill Avenue, Nita City, Nita	unknown

5 NARRATIVE

regarding any connection that Burns might have to the Carletti murder, would result in accepting a plea to lesser charges from Jones, presumably accepting a plea to Robbery and dropping of the Murder charges. The District Attorney, Anthony Alifano, instructed me to get an arrest warrant for Burns for Robbery and Murder and to execute the warrant as soon as possible. Warrant was obtained on 5/11/YR-0 at 6:00 p.m. from Judge Beckman and was executed immediately. Burns was placed under arrest at 6:30 p.m. at his residence at 221 Elm Street, Nita City, Nita.

5/12/YR-0—Continued investigation in the above matter. Spoke to District Attorney Anthony Alifano concerning possible plea bargain from Jones in return for testimony. Mr. Alifano authorized me to tell defendant Jones that in return for truthful testimony regarding Mr. Burns's involvement in the Carletti murder he would dismiss the pending murder charge with leave to reinstate should Jones lie on the stand and accept a guilty plea to the Robbery. Following this conversation with Mr. Alifano, I again spoke to the defendant Jones. He again agreed to talk to me and I communicated Mr. Alifano's offer. He agreed to cooperate only if Alifano put his offer in writing which I assured Jones would occur. Then took Jones to the courtroom where Burns was about the be arraigned. Burns was sitting in the front row of the courtroom between two uniformed officers. There was no one else present in the courtroom. Jones looked in through the window and I asked him if he recognized anyone and he told me that Burns was the man who had picked him up in the green Cutlass on May 9, YR-0. I then asked Jones if he would give another statement and he indicated that he would.

6 OFFICER'S NAME	7 OFFICER'S SIGNATURE
Det. Arthur Hellman	Det. Arthur Hellman

8 DATE/SUBMITTED MO DAY YR	TIME 24 Hour Clock	9 SUPERVISOR'S NAME	10
5/12/YR-0	300	J. McCormick	Page 4 of 4

NITA CITY POLICE DEPARTMENT
NITA CITY, NITA

ARREST REPORT

1 ARREST NUMBER	2 PRINTS [X] PHOTOS [X]	3 NAME LAST	FIRST	MIDDLE
3197-YR-0		Burns	John	NMI

4 ALIAS/NICKNAME	5 DATE OF BIRTH	6 AGE	7 SEX	8 RACE/ETHNIC
N/A	9/4/YR-35	35	M	C

9 ADDRESS	PHONE	10 PLACE OF BIRTH
221 Elm Street, Nita City, Nita	493-4143	Meriden, Nita

11 HEIGHT	12 WEIGHT	13 HAIR	14 EYES	15 COMPLEXION	16 SOC. SEC. NUMBER
5' 10"	175	Brown	Hazel	Fair/clear	045-38-6262

17 OPERATOR LICENSE NUMBER & STATE	18 MISCELLANEOUS	19 OCCUPATION
N-3132418		unemployed

20 EMPLOYEE/SCHOOL	21 ADDRESS	PHONE
N/A	N/A	N/A

DETAILS OF ARREST

22 DATE OF ARREST MO DAY YR	23 TIME 24 hr clock	24 HOW ARRESTED
5/11/YR-0	1830	ON VIEW [ ] WARRANT [X] ORDER FOR ARREST [ ]

25 PLACE OF ARREST: 221 Elm Street, Nita City, Nita

26 INITIAL CHARGE	27 COUNTS	28 STATUTE	29 OFFENSE JURISDICTION	30 WARRANT DATE MO DAY YR
Murder	1	18-6-102 (1)(b)	Nita City & Darrow County	5/11/YR-0

31 SUBSEQUENT CHARGE	32 COUNTS	33 STATUTE	34 OFFENSE JURISDICTION	35 WARRANT DATE MO DAY YR
Armed robbery	1	18-6-302	Nita City & Darrow County	5/11/YR-0

36 VEHICLE INFORMATION				37 PLACE STORED
LICENSE # N/A	STATE N/A	MAKE N/A	VIN N/A	N/A

38 VEHICLE INVENTORY INFORMATION MO DAY YR BY: N/A

39 COMPLAINANT'S NAME	ADDRESS	PHONE
James Silvio Carletti	61 Hill Avenue, Nita City, Nita	unknown

CONFINEMENT/BOND INFORMATION

40 DATE CONFINED MO DAY YR	TIME 24 Hour Clock	41 PLACE CONFINED	42 COMMITTING MAGISTRATE
5/11/YR-0	1830	Nita City Jail	Gregory S. Lewis

43 TYPE BOND	44 AMOUNT	45 DATE RELEASED MO DAY YR	TIME 24 HOUR CLOCK	46 RELEASED BY
None	N/A			N/A

DISPOSITION INFORMATION

47 DEPOSITION DATE MO DAY YR	48 COURT DOCKET	49 COURT/JUDGE	CITY
	YR-0-CR-324	Darrow County-Superior Court	in Nita City

50 DISPOSITION	51 SENTENCE

52 NARRATIVE On 5/11/YR-0, I obtained an arrest warrant for the defendant from Judge Beckman at 6:00 p.m. The warrant was executed by me at 6:30 p.m. on the same date at the home of the defendant Burns at 221 Elm Street, Nita City, Nitz. The defendant offered no resistance Also present at the scene of the arrest was the defendant's wife Mary N. Burns. I informed defendant that he was under arrest for the murder of Teresa B. Carletti on 5/9/YR-0 at 401 Main Street, Nita City, Nita. I

RIGHT THUMB

53 ARRESTING OFFICER -- NAME AND SIGNATURE	54 DATE/SUBMITTED MO DAY YR	TIME 24 Hour Clock
Det. Arthur Hellman, NCPD		

55 SUPERVISOR SIGNATURE	56 ARRESTEE SIGNATURE
J. McCormick	

NITA CITY POLICE DEPARTMENT
NITA CITY, NITA

ARREST REPORT—CONTINUATION PAGE

1 ARREST NUMBER	2 NAME LAST	FIRST	MIDDLE	3 ALIAS/NICKNAME
3197-YR-0	Burns	John	NMI	N/A

4 COMPLAINANT'S NAME	ADDRESS	PHONE
James Silvio Carletti	61 Hill Avenue, Nita City, Nita	unknown

5 NARRATIVE

informed the defendant of his Miranda rights and asked him if he understood them. He said that he did. His wife protested that her husband had been home all day Saturday. I told her she could come down to the police station and make a statement if she wanted to. I took the defendant into custody and brought him down to the station. After he was booked, I asked the defendant Burns if he wanted to talk about it. He responded that he didn't know what I was talking about but that he was more than willing to talk about it because he did not have anything to hide. I informed the defendant Burns of the basic facts of the charges against him. He did not seem to react one way or the other. I then again informed him of his rights and he said that he understood them and would be more than happy to tell me what he was doing on the afternoon of Saturday, May 9th. He said that he had two alibi witnesses, his wife and a friend, Larry Roberts. Defendant was brought before Magistrate Lewis who denied bond. Defendant was placed in the lock-up for the night.

5/12/YR-0—Investigation continued in the above matter. Defendant was taken out of the lock-up shortly before 9:00 a.m. and taken into the empty District Court courtroom by two uniformed officers. The three men sat in the front row of the courtroom spectator section. Lauren Jones was brought to the window of the courtroom to ascertain if he could identify the defendant Burns. Jones made a positive identification of Burns as the man with whom he had planned the robbery of Carletti IGA Market. The defendant was then arraigned on Murder and Robbery charges. Later that afternoon the defendant's wife, Mary N. Burns, and friend, Lawrence Roberts, arrived at the station. They both insisted on making statements that were typed out and sworn to before a notary public.

6 OFFICER'S NAME	7 OFFICER'S SIGNATURE
Det. Arthur Hellman	Det. Arthur Hellman

8 DATE/SUBMITTED MO DAY YR	TIME 24 Hour Clock	9 SUPERVISOR'S NAME	10
5/13/YR-0		J. McCormick	Page 2 of 2

STATEMENT OF JAMES S. CARLETTI**

My name is James S. Carletti. I live at 61 Hill Avenue, Nita City, Nita. I am 58 years old. This afternoon, May 9, YR-0, a man tried to rob our store. The name of our store is Carletti's IGA Market and it's located at 401 Main St., Nita City, Nita. As I said, a man tried to rob our store. He was the same man who was arrested there just a little while ago. He came into the store wearing ordinary street clothes with a blue and white bandana on his face. He had a gun in his hand. He said he wanted all the money out of the register. He got in a hurry and pushed the cash button on my register and reached in and grabbed the bills in the top drawer of the register. I then reached under the counter and grabbed a pistol I had bought for protection and came up real fast and fired a shot. Somehow he had gotten out of the way and the shot hit Teresa. He yelled something about his gun not being loaded. I told him not to move or I'd kill him and ran over to Teresa. She was bleeding really bad. She said, "It was the same car, the same man." She then said some really personal things that I'd rather not say. I believe her first statement meant that the car and the man in the car that was parked outside the store, right in front of the window, facing the wrong way, was the same car she had told me about several times during the past week. She had said that she thought that a man in a green, fairly new American car was planning to rob the store because it kept driving by the store real slow. I didn't think much of it at the time. Maybe if I had listened to her she'd still be alive.

That's all I can remember right now; if you could, please leave me alone.

Name: James Carletti

Date: May 9, YR-0

Witness: Det. Arthur Hellman

Witness: Walter Dellinger

Date: May 9, YR-0

**This statement was given to Detective Arthur Hellman at Walter Dellinger's house immediately after the robbery.

STATEMENT OF LAUREN JONES**

My name is Lauren Jones. I live at 3800 Hillgrand Drive, Nita City, Nita. I am 28 years old. On May 9, YR-0, I attempted to rob the IGA Market on the corner of Fourth and Main in Nita City, Nita. During the course of that attempt, the owner of the store pulled out a gun from under the cash register counter and tried to shoot me. I ducked, and he shot and killed his wife. Even though I had a gun with me, I did not attempt to fire it. The owner of the store kept me face down on the floor until the police came and arrested me.

I bought the gun from a man who I did not know. The purchase took place in a bar in New City, Nita, the night before. On May 9, which was a Saturday, I hitchhiked from New City to Nita City on Route 40, which is a distance of about 15 miles. It took several rides to reach Nita City. I did not know any of the people who picked me up. The last ride was in a late model green Oldsmobile. I had the driver leave me off in front of the IGA that I tried to rob. I never intended to hurt anyone; I just needed the money because I am unemployed and I can't get any more money from the State.

NAME: Lauren Jones

DATE: May 9, YR-0

SUBSCRIBED AND SWORN TO before me this 9th day of May, YR-0.

Anne Dolan

Notary Public

**This statement was given to Detective Arthur Hellman at the Nita City Police Station the evening of May 9th.

STATEMENT OF LAUREN JONES**

My name is Lauren Jones. I live at 3800 Hillgrand Drive, Nita City, Nita. I am 28 years old. I am making this statement because I want to. I have been told what my rights are and I want to give them up and make this statement. On May 9, YR-0, I was involved in an attempted robbery at the IGA Market on the corner of Fourth and Main. I gave an earlier statement about all this which was not true because I was scared. This is the complete truth.

On May 9th, I was picked up at the corner of Elm and Fourth by John Burns. I knew John Burns back from when we were in prison together a lot of years ago. We weren't real close then, but we had run into each other in a bar in Nita City about two weeks before all this happened. We talked some about the days in prison and about how hard it was for ex-cons to find work. I think the name of the bar was McSorley's. Burnsey told me about a plan he had to hold up a grocery store. He said the guy who owned it was old and kept lots of cash around. Burnsey said the only problem was that he had been around casing the place and he was afraid that the owner would recognize him if he pulled it off. He talked me into doing it for him. He said he would drive the job. We talked about when to do it and he said a Saturday would be best and that he would call me when he was ready. I gave him my phone number.

On Saturday the 9th, he called and told me to be on the corner at Fourth and Elm at 3:00 p.m. and to stay there until he got there. When he picked me up, I got into the right front seat. It was sometime between 3:30 and 4:00 p.m. I'm not real sure about the time. Burns started to drive around while we talked. He reached over into the glove compartment, took out a gun and a blue bandana, and handed it to me. I told him that I didn't want a gun. He had said the job was going to be easy; why did I need a gun? He told me that it was just in case. He showed me that the firing pin had been removed and that there were no shells in it. He said the gun was just to scare the old people.

We pulled by the store once to make sure there were no customers there. Burnsey pulled the car up on the wrong side of the street in front of the store. The car was a pretty new, green Oldsmobile. I put the bandana on before I got out of the car. I went into the store with the gun in my belt. I didn't pull the gun out until I got inside. Everything else happened the way I

**This statement was given to Detective Arthur Hellman at the Nita City Police Station.

said in my first statement, except that after the old man shot his wife, I heard him pull away in a real hurry. That is what happened.

NAME: Lauren Jones

DATE: May 11, YR-0

SUBSCRIBED AND SWORN TO before me this 11th day of May, YR-0.

Anne Dolan

Notary Public

STATE OF NITA	)	IN THE SUPERIOR COURT OF
	)	DARROW COUNTY
v.	)	STATE OF NITA
	)	
JOHN BURNS	)	

May 19, YR-0

PRELIMINARY HEARING
TRANSCRIPT OF PROCEEDINGS

Clerk: Oyez, Oyez, Oyez, Superior Court for Darrow County is now open and in session. All those having cause before this court draw nigh and give their attention according to law. God save the Court and the State of Nita. The Honorable John Perkins presiding. Good morning, your Honor.

Court: Good morning. What's the first case on the docket this morning?

Clerk: Your Honor, we have a preliminary hearing in the case of State v. John Burns.

Court: Very well, is the State ready?

Prosecutor: Yes, your Honor.

Court: What are the charges here?

Prosecutor: Your Honor, the defendant is charged with violation of Nita General Statutes 18-6-302 and 18-3-102(1)(b).

Court: Will the defendant rise? Mr. Burns, you are charged with violation of Nita General Statutes 18-6-302 and 18-3-102(1)(b). How do you plead to these charges?

Def. Att'y: The Defendant pleads not guilty to both charges.

Court: A plea of not guilty will be entered. The State may call its first witness.

Prosecutor: The State calls James Silvio Carletti.

Court: Mr. Carletti, come around. Please raise your right hand. Do you swear that the testimony you are about to give will be the truth, the whole truth, and nothing but the truth?

Carletti: I do, so help me God.

Prosecutor: Would you state your name and address for the record, please?

A: James Silvio Carletti, 61 Hill Avenue, Nita City, Nita.

Q: Are you employed?

A: Yes, I own Carletti's IGA Market on the corner of Main and Fourth in Nita City, Nita.

Q: Where do you pay your property taxes?

A: I pay them at the Darrow County Tax Assessor's Office. Both my home and market are in Nita City and Darrow County.

Q: How long have you owned your business?

A: For 20 years. I used to work nights as a second job for Mr. Goldstein, the former owner, and when he retired, I bought the business from him. My wife and I ran the business and I quit the job that I had at the steel mill where I had worked for 17 years.

Q: Did your wife work before you bought the market?

A: No, she was busy raising the five kids.

Q: Directing your attention to Saturday, May 9, YR-0, can you tell us what transpired at about 4:00 p.m.?

A: Teresa and I were alone in the store. I was cleaning up the counter area and she was arranging some magazines in the magazine rack that backs up on the front window. That's usually a slow time at the store and we were going to close at 5:00 p.m. for the weekend so we wanted to tidy up so we'd be ready for business on Monday morning. Right about that time, a man came in the store and pointed a gun at me and told me to clean out the cash register. He reached around, opened the register, and took the cash from the top of the drawer. I was real upset because we had all of Friday and Saturday's receipts, which amounted to over $900, underneath the cash drawer. I reached under the counter and pulled out the gun that I had bought for protection and fired one shot real quick. The guy had ducked out of the way. His hand opened and the money dropped back on the open register drawer. The bullet hit Teresa. Teresa screamed and fell to the floor. The robber was on the floor too, and I told him not to move or I'd kill him. I ran over to Teresa and held her in my arms. There was blood all over the place.

Q: Did she say anything to you?

A: Yes, she said, "It was the same car, the same man." She then said that she always loved me and told me to take care of myself and the children. Then she smiled, closed her eyes, and died in my arms.

Q: What did her last words mean to you?

A: Well, we had been held up twice in the past year — once in January and once in April. That's why I bought the gun; I wish I never had; and Teresa was real nervous about being robbed again. She had told me on several occasions during the week before she died that a fairly new, green American car had driven by the store real slow. She told me that she thought the driver was planning to rob the store. I didn't think much of it at the time, thinking Teresa was being overly suspicious, but I guess she was right. I guess she saw the defendant.

Q: What did you do then?

A: Well, I was crying and I wanted to kill the robber who was still on the floor, but I didn't. I called the police and they got there in a few minutes. I talked to an officer; I was still real upset. They took the robber away.

Q: Looking around the courtroom, can you identify the man who tried to rob your store?

A: Yes, that's him over there.

Q: Your Honor, may the record indicate that the witness has identified Lauren Jones as the man who tried to rob his store on May 9, YR-0?

Court: Any objection?

Def. Att'y: No, your Honor.

Court: The record will so indicate. Mr. Prosecutor, you may proceed.

Prosecutor: Thank you, your Honor. Mr. Carletti, do you remember seeing a green late-model American car near the time of the robbery?

A: Oh yes, I forgot to tell you. The man who tried to rob the store got out of a late-model green American car before he came into the store. I noticed it only because the car drove up to the store and parked on the wrong side of the street right in front of the store. The robber got out of the passenger side and walked around the car into the store. I never saw the car after that. I guess the driver got scared and took off.

Q: Did you see the driver?

A: Yes, I got a glimpse of his face. He was on the side of the car nearest to me.

Q: Looking around the courtroom, do you see the driver of the car here today?

A: Well, I'm not sure, but I think it's that guy over there (pointing).

Prosecutor: May the record reflect the witness has identified the defendant?

Court: Any objection?

Def. Att'y: Not at this time.

Court: Very well, the record will so reflect.

Q: Mr. Carletti, had you ever fired your gun before May 9, YR-0?

A: No, not before or since. I had bought it only a month before the robbery because the police were never there to protect us when we needed them. Now Teresa is dead.

Prosecutor: I have no further questions of this witness at this time, your Honor.

Def. Att'y: I move for production of any statements of this witness in the possession of the State.

Prosecutor: There is one statement which the State will provide to the defense.

Court: Any cross examination?

Def. Att'y: Yes, just a few questions. Mr. Carletti, I notice that you're wearing glasses. Did you have your glasses on the date of this incident?

A: Yes, I always do.

Q: Is your vision corrected to 20-20?

A: Yes, it is.

Q: Did your wife wear glasses?

A: No, she had perfect vision.

Q: Did you see the driver of this green car?

A: Yes, and I'm sure my wife did, too.

Q: Did you see the license plate of the green car?

A: Well, some of it.

Q: What exactly did you see?

A: It was a Nita license and I could make out one letter and one number.

Q: What were they?

A: "K" and an "8."

Q: Where were they on the license plate?

A: I don't know.

Q: How far were you from the driver?

A: About 20 feet.

Q: How long did you look at him?

A: Only a second or two.

Q: Mr. Carletti, you strike me as an honest man. Isn't it true that you're not sure the defendant is the man who was in the car?

A: I'm not positive, if that's what you mean. It looks like him, but I'm just not sure.

Q: Did you give a description of the man to the police?

A: No, they never asked for one and I was too shaken to think of it.

Q: How far was your wife from the driver?

A: The car couldn't have been more than ten feet away from where she was standing.

Q: Did the magazine rack obstruct her view?

A: No, the rack is only four feet tall and she was 5'5" tall, a beautiful woman.

Q: Were the windows clean?

A: Yes, Teresa washed them every day.

Q: Do you know the defendant?

A: No, I don't.

Def. Att'y: I have no further questions, your Honor.

Prosecutor: Nothing further for the State with this witness, your Honor.

Court: Very well, you may be excused, Mr. Carletti. Does the State have any further witnesses?

Prosecutor: Yes, your Honor, the State calls Lauren Jones.

Court: Come around, Mr. Jones. Do you swear that the testimony which you're about to give will be the truth, the whole truth, and nothing but the truth?

Mr. Jones: I do.

Prosecutor: State your name and address for the record.

A: Lauren Jones, 3800 Hillgrand Drive, Nita City, Nita.

Q: Are you married?

A: No, never.

Q: Are you employed?

A: No, not at this time.

Q: How do you usually occupy yourself?

A: Since the Army, I've worked odd jobs, nothing permanent.

Q: Directing your attention to May 9, YR-0, at about 3:30 p.m., can you tell the court what you were doing?

A: Yes, I was waiting on the corner of Elm and Fourth for someone to pick me up.

Q: Were you picked up?

A: Yes, John Burns, he's a guy who had done time at the State Pen while I was there, came by in a YR-1 green Oldsmobile Cutlass between 3:30 and 4:00.

Q: Why were you waiting for him?

A: Burnsey and I had run into each other several weeks before in a local bar. We hadn't seen each other since prison. After talking about how good it was to be out, we complained to each other about how rough it was for cons to get jobs. He told me that he really needed some money to help support his family and that he had staked out a grocery store in Nita City that would be easy pickings. Burnsey told me that if I would help him do the job, he'd split the money even. He said the reason he needed help was that he had cased the place too many times and he thought the people who owned it might recognize him if he pulled the job. I was really broke, so I agreed to do it.

Q: What happened after he picked you up?

A: Burnsey drove around for a few minutes. He reached over and pulled a gun and a blue bandana out of his glove compartment. He told me the gun didn't work because the firing pin had been removed, but that I wouldn't have any trouble because the owners were two old people who would be scared stiff just by seeing the gun.

Q: What did you do then?

A: Well, we cruised by the store once to make sure that there were no customers who might get in the way. I put the bandana on and took the gun. Burnsey pulled over in front of the store, parking on the wrong side of the street right next to the store. I got out of the car, walked around it and into the store.

Q: Who was in the store?

A: Just like he said, there was an old man behind the cash register and an old lady standing near the magazine rack next to the window. I went up to the old man and told him to give me everything out of the cash register. He didn't move, so I hit the cash button and grabbed the money out of the top of the cash drawer. The old man then reached under the counter and I figured that he was going for a gun. I knew that my gun didn't work so I dropped the money and hit the deck. I heard one shot fired and the old lady scream. I yelled at the old man that my gun wasn't loaded. He told me not to move or he'd kill me, so I stayed put. He went over to the old lady and started talking to her. I couldn't hear what they were saying. The old man then came over to me and told me again not to move or I was a dead man. He called the cops and I could hear that he was crying. I guess he killed his wife when he shot. The cops came and arrested me.

Q: What happened to the YR-1 Cutlass?

A: Right after I heard the shot, I heard some tires screech, so I guess he just took off.

Q: Have you been charged with any offense for your activities on May 9, YR-0?

A: Yes, I pleaded guilty to robbery, yesterday, May 18th.

Q: Looking around the courtroom, do you see the man who was driving the YR-1 Cutlass?

A: Yes, that's Burnsey right over there.

Prosecutor: May the record reflect that the witness has identified the defendant, John Burns?

Court: Any objection?

Def. Att'y: No objection, your Honor.

Court: The record will so reflect. Does the State have anything further?

Prosecutor: We have no further questions of this witness at this time, your Honor.

Court: Does the defense have any cross examination?

Def. Att'y: Just a few questions, your Honor, but first we would move that the State produce any statements of this witness in its possession.

Prosecutor: Your Honor, there are two statements that I will provide to the defense attorney.

Court: Very well, let's proceed with cross examination.

Def. Att'y: Mr. Jones, what is your social security number?

A: 049-36-4748

Q: Did you spend any time in the military?

A: Yes, I was in the Army after I graduated from high school here in Nita City.

Q: What type of discharge did you receive?

A: It was a dishonorable discharge; they trumped up some charges against me, saying that I ripped off the PX, but I was clean.

Q: Isn't it true, Mr. Jones, that you were originally charged with murder as well as robbery in this case?

A: Yes, the murder charge was dropped. Look it, my gun wasn't even loaded. The old man shot his wife, not me.

Q: You have entered a guilty plea on the robbery charge, isn't that correct?

A: Yes, I already said that.

Q: Have you been sentenced on that charge?

A: No, not yet.

Q: When will that happen?

A: I don't know, they haven't told me.

Q: Are you currently being held in jail?

A: No, I made bond; my brother put up his house.

Q: Since you got out of jail, had you ever seen my client before today?

A: Sure, three times — once when we met in the bar; once on the day of the robbery, like I said; and then the Tuesday after I got busted. Burnsey was sitting in a courtroom between two uniformed cops; they were the only ones there. I looked in and identified him as the guy who got me in all this trouble, the guy in the green Cutlass.

Q: Did you tell the police about the man in the green car immediately after they arrested you?

A: No, it wasn't until after I got arraigned on Monday, May 11, YR-0.

Q: Why did you wait until then?

A: Because when I was in the car with Burnsey, he told me that he was connected, you know, had some tough friends, and said that the holdup was a piece of cake, but that if I screwed up and got caught that I better forget that I ever saw him and that if I said anything about him that it would be a real mistake and I believed him because he had a real tough reputation in the joint.

Q: Mr. Jones, how many times have you been convicted of criminal offenses?

Prosecutor: Your Honor, at this point I'll have to object. Mr. Jones's criminal record is a matter of public record that counsel can easily obtain and I don't believe that inquiry at this point is necessary or relevant to determining probable cause to hold the defendant for trial.

Court: Objection sustained.

Def. Att'y: I have no further questions, your Honor.

Prosecutor: No redirect, your Honor.

Court: You may be excused, Mr. Jones. Does the State have any further witnesses?

Prosecutor: Just one, your Honor. The State calls Detective Arthur Hellman.

Court: Detective Hellman, do you swear that the testimony that you are about to give will be the truth, the whole truth, and nothing but the truth?

Hellman: I do.

Court: Very well, you may proceed.

Prosecutor: Could you state your name and badge number for the record?

A: I'm Detective Arthur Hellman, Badge No. 914, Nita City P.D.

Q: Where do you live?

A: 712 Hall Avenue, Nita City, Nita.

Q: How old are you?

A: 33.

Q: How long have you been with the Nita City P.D.?

A: Eleven years.

Q: What did you do before you joined the force?

A: After I graduated from high school in YR-15, I did a four-year hitch in the Navy from which I received an honorable discharge in YR-11. It was right after that that I joined the Nita City P.D.

Q: Are you married?

A: Yes, I've been married to the former Nancy Martin for ten years. We have two children — Jeff, who's nine; and Jennifer, who's seven.

Q: Have you always been a detective?

A: No, I started out as a patrolman and worked my way up through the ranks. I became a detective three years ago.

Q: Have you received any special training while on the force?

A: Yes, just before I was promoted to detective, I attended the FBI school in Washington, DC. Since I was scheduled to join the burglary squad, I received special training in fingerprint analysis, including both the techniques of removing prints from suspicious objects and the analysis of those prints once they have been removed.

Q: Directing your attention to May 9, YR-0, did you have occasion to investigate an alleged robbery and murder at Carletti's IGA Market at 401 Main Street, Nita City, Nita?

A: Yes, I was the chief investigating officer.

Q: Can you briefly relate what occurred that afternoon?

A: Yes, may I refer to my reports?

Prosecutor: With leave of the Court.

Court: Does the defense have any objection to the detective referring to his reports?

Def. Att'y: I have no objection, your Honor.

Court: Very well, you may refer to your reports, Detective Hellman.

Hellman: Thank you, your Honor.

Court: You may proceed.

Prosecutor: Again, Detective, can you briefly state what occurred on the afternoon of May 9, YR-0?

A: I was called to the Carletti IGA Market at about 4:15 p.m. Upon arrival, I noted that Mr. Carletti was holding a gun on a man later identified as Lauren Jones. Mrs. Carletti was lying in a pool of blood near the magazine rack next to the front window. I checked her and she appeared to be dead. Mr. Carletti informed me that Jones had tried to rob him and that he, Carletti, had attempted to shoot Jones, had missed, and hit his wife. I put Mr. Jones under arrest and took Mr. Carletti's gun, a .22 caliber pistol, from him and took from Mr. Jones a .38 caliber Smith & Wesson pistol, and put both weapons in individual evidence bags. I was very careful not to smudge any possible prints on either weapon. I took Mr. Carletti to his neighbor's house while other officers took Jones downtown. Mr. Carletti gave me a statement there.

Q: Did you test the .38 for fingerprints?

A: Yes, I found a complete set of prints from Jones' right hand and one unidentifiable print on the barrel of the weapon just forward of the firing mechanism which I later found to be the left thumb print of the defendant, John Burns.

Q: How did you connect Burns with this weapon?

A: On Monday, May 11, YR-0, I phoned the Nita Weapon Registration Department and found that the .38 pistol was registered to Mary N. Burns, the defendant's wife. I also found that Mr. Burns, the defendant, owned a green YR-1 Oldsmobile Cutlass that was allegedly involved in the robbery. I then checked to see if Burns had a record, found that he did, pulled his fingerprint card, and compared it to the previously unidentified print. The left thumbprint on the card and gun matched perfectly.

Q: What did you do then?

A: I obtained an arrest warrant for John Burns and executed the warrant and took him into custody at 6:30 p.m. that night.

Q: Has anything else of importance happened in regard to this case?

A: Yes, on Tuesday, May 12, YR-0, Mr. Jones identified the defendant Burns as the man who helped him plan the robbery of the IGA Market on May 9th. Also, Mrs. Burns and friends of Mr. Burns' came down to the station on the same day and gave statements.

Prosecutor: I have no further questions of this witness.

Court: Any cross examination?

Def. Att'y: Your Honor, we would move for production of the reports that the detective used in making his testimony.

Court: Motion is granted.

Def. Att'y: We have no questions of this witness, your Honor.

Court: You may be excused, Detective. Does the State have any more witnesses?

Prosecutor: No, your Honor. At this time we would move that the defendant John Burns be bound over to the Superior Court for trial on the charges of Murder in violation of G.S. 18-3-102(1)(b) and Armed Robbery in violation of G.S. 18-6-302.

Court: The Court finds probable cause on both charges and orders that the defendant John Burns be held for trial without bail on both charges.

THE NITA MORNING GLOBE
May 10, YR-0, Page 1

Man Misses Robber, Kills Wife

NITA CITY, Nita--Firing at a hold-up man, James S. Carletti missed his target and the bullet struck his wife, Teresa, who died in his arms moments later.

The Carlettis, co-owners of the IGA Grocery at Fourth and Main, were alone in the store when a masked robber entered. A sobbing Carletti later told reporters, "After the second robbery this year, I went out and bought a gun. When the punk told me to give him all my money, I told him I would. He reached for the money in the cash register and I reached for my gun under the counter." Carletti, overcome by grief, was unable to conclude his account of the robbery.

Detective Arthur Hellman of the Nita City Police, the first to arrive at the scene, provided additional details, "Apparently Carletti had never fired the gun before. The poor guy shot his wife who was putting magazines on the shelf by the front window."

Hellman said police believe Carletti kept the robber pinned down at the same time he rushed to his wife's aid. Police officials have identified the suspect in custody as Lauren Jones of Nita City and have indicated he will be charged with first degree murder and robbery.

No charges will be filed against Carletti.

Teresa Carletti spoke to her husband for a few moments before she died. Both Carletti and Detective Hellman have declined comment on what she said.

Teresa Carletti was pronounced dead at the scene by Coroner Fred Rothman at 4:28 p.m.

TERESA CARLETTI

Teresa Bianco Carletti, 55, a Nita City Resident for 35 years, died yesterday from a gunshot wound received during a hold-up of the IGA Grocery store she and her husband owned and operated.

Both Mrs. Carletti and her husband, James, were born in Milan, Italy. Married in YR-37, Mrs. Carletti's husband left Italy in YR-36 for the United States. After working in this country for a year he was able to pay her fare to Nita City. The family lives at 61 Hill Avenue.

For 17 years Mrs. Carletti raised children and was a housewife. Her husband worked days at the Mammouth Steel Mill and nights at Goldstein's IGA Grocery.

In YR-19 the Carlettis purchased the grocery store from the retiring Abraham Goldstein. Mrs. C, as she was known by regular customers, worked side by side with her husband in the business. In YR-3 the couple added to the store doubling its original size.

Long active in community affairs, the deceased was a founder of the Women's Auxiliary of the Libero Pensiero Club which her husband formerly headed. The Club and its Women's Auxiliary sponsored the annual fund drive for the Nita County Children's Hospital.

Mrs. Carletti was also an active member of Our Lady of Fatima Church and president of the Altar Society which helped maintain the interior of the building and provide flowers for Sunday services.

Two years ago, Mrs. Carletti achieved a life long goal by passing the citizenship test and becoming an American citizen. Her husband became a citizen seven years after his arrival in this country.

The deceased is survived by her husband, five children and five grandchildren. Her twins, age 29, are Anthony J. Carletti, a priest in Hoboken, N.J., and Mary C. Procacci, an attorney and mother of two children in Westport, Nita. Daughter Terri C. Lang, 27, a housewife and mother of three children, lives in Groton, Nita. Richard X. Carletti, 25, is a management trainee with IBM and lives in White Plains, NY. He is married to the former Susan Conti of Yalesville. Constance N. Carletti, 24, is a student at the University of Nita School of Medicine in Farmington.

The family requests that donations in lieu of flowers be sent to Our Lady of Fatima Church.

THE NITA MORNING GLOBE
May 9, YR-0, Page 18

TODAY'S SPORTS
ON TELEVISION

4:00 (8) Wide World of Sports. Live from Las Vegas the Invitational Bowling Tournament, $150,000 in prize money and America's best bowlers. Keith Jackson and Don Carter, 120 mins.

EXHIBIT — Map of Nita City, Nita

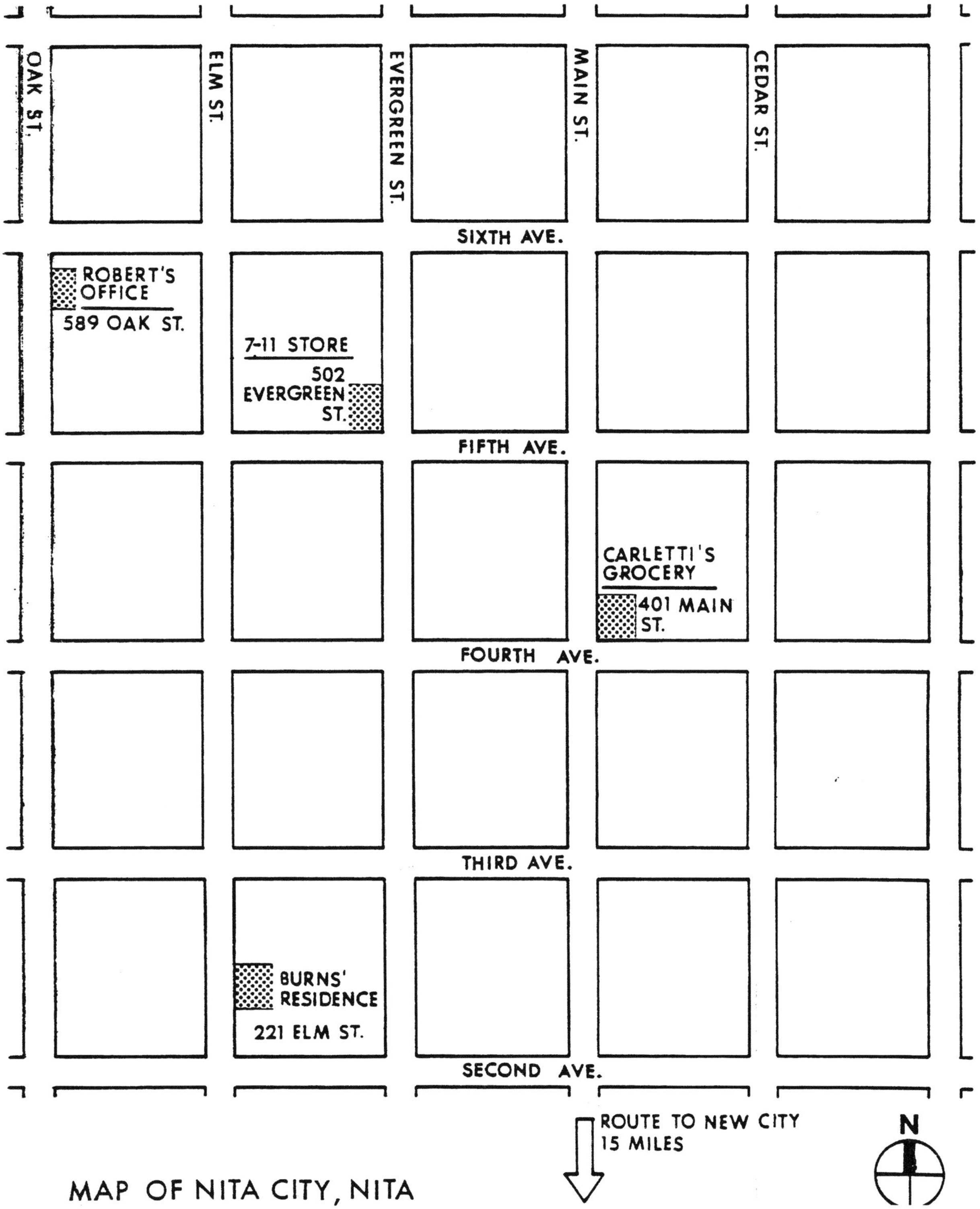

EXHIBIT — Diagram of Carletti's IGA Market

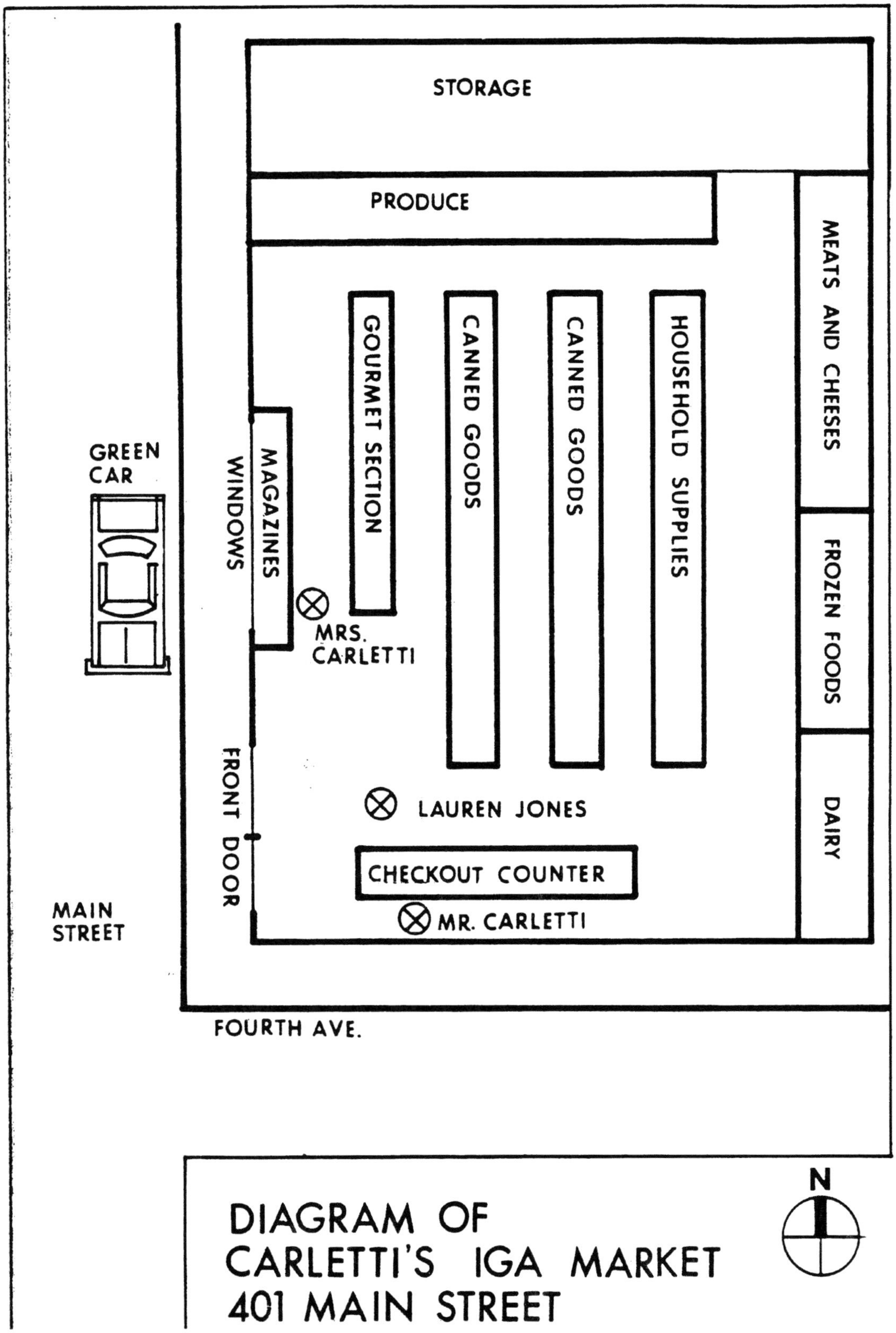

EXHIBIT — Floor Plan of Burn's Residence at 221 Elm Street

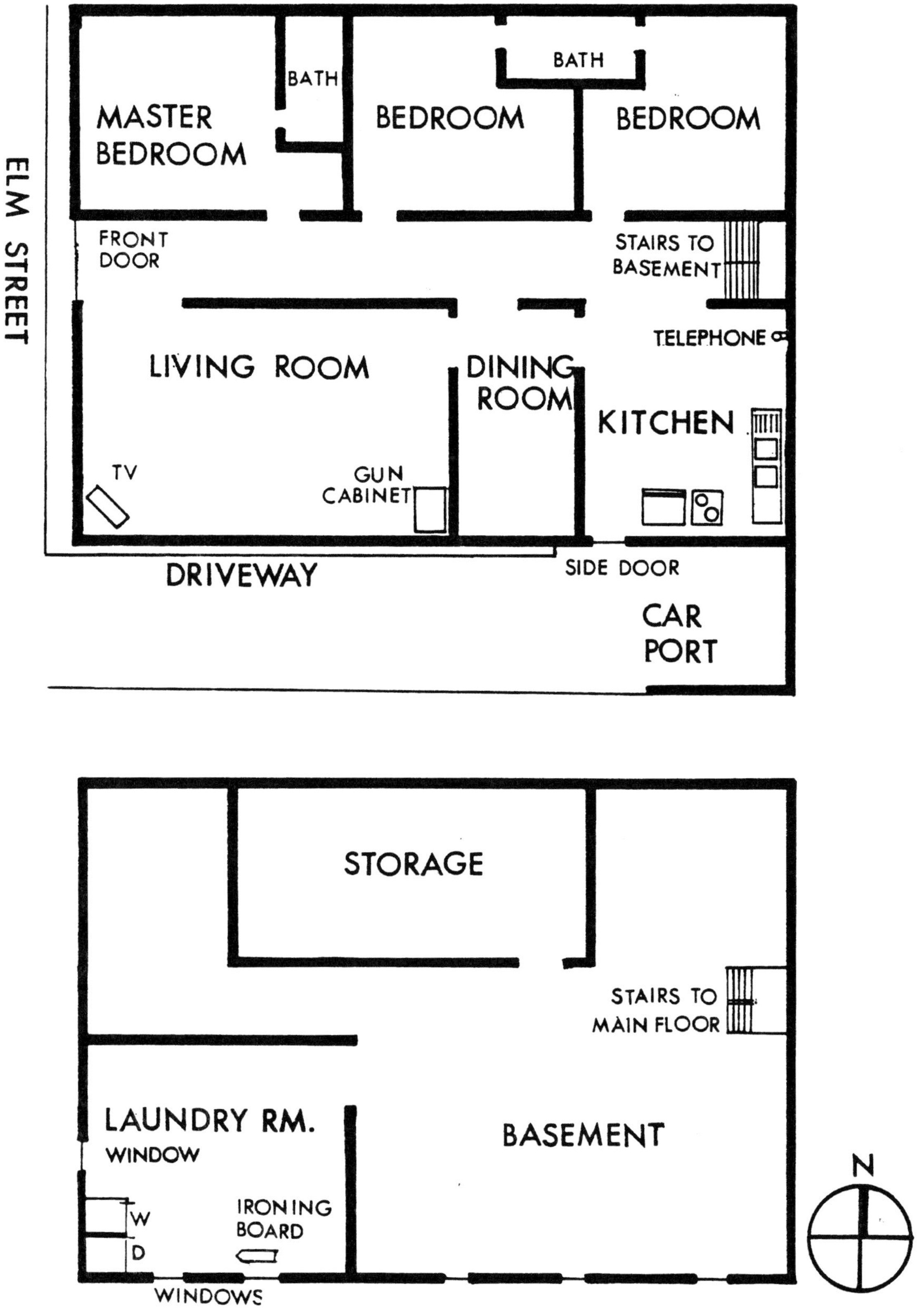

FLOOR PLAN OF BURNS RESIDENCE AT 221 ELM STREET

UNIFORM ARREST AND DISPOSITION RECORD

NAME: Lauren Jones		DOB: 7/31/YR-28	
SS. NO. 049-36-4748		POB: Meriden, Nita	
DATE	ADDRESS	OFFENSE	DISPOSITION
2/24/YR-14	707 Williams St. Nita City, Nita	18-15-409 Joyriding	Adj. delinquent Probation 2 yrs.
5/28/YR-13	600 Asylum Avenue Nita City, Nita	18-12-105 Carrying concealed weapon	Prob. violation 1 yr. Training School Released 3/14/YR-12.
9/22/YR-11	735 Clarkson St. Nita City, Nita	18-7-202 First Degree Burglary	Plea to 2nd degree 2-5 yr. State Penitentiary. Paroled 4/10/YR-9.
11/14/YR-9	37 Bainton Road Nita City, Nita	18-6-301 Robbery	5-10 yrs. State Penitentiary. Paroled 2/8/YR-5.
4/17/YR-5	925 25th St. Nita City, Nita	18-7-202 First Degree Burglary	10-20 yrs. State Penitentiary. Paroled 8/4/YR-1.
5/9/YR-0	3800 Hillgrand Dr. Nita City, Nita	18-3-102 (1)(b) Murder 18-6-302 Armed Robbery	Dismissed with leave. Plea of guilty.

Alexander McConachie

Alexander McConachie
Superintendent of Documents

Certified as of this 13th day of May, YR-0.

Charlotte Noll

Charlotte Noll, Notary Public

UNIFORM ARREST AND DISPOSITION RECORD

NAME: John Burns		DOB: 9/4/YR-35	
SS. NO. 045-38-6262		POB: Meriden, Nita	
DATE	ADDRESS	OFFENSE	DISPOSITION
2/18/YR-13	2112 York Ave., Apt. 21 Nita City, Nita	7-2-104(b) Poss. Heroin with Intent to Sell 7-2-194(a) Poss. Heroin	Dismissed w/o leave Plead Guilty 2-5 yrs. Paroled State Penitentiary 5/12/YR-12
12/3/YR-9	412 N. Salem Nita City, Nita	7-2-194(a) Poss. Heroin	Plead Guilty 2-5 yr. Paroled State Penitentiary 11/7/YR-8
4/21/YR-4	221 Elm Street Nita City, Nita	18-10-105 Gambling	Dismissed with leave
9/14/YR-4	221 Elm Street Nita City, Nita	18-10-105 Gambling	Dismissed with leave
11/17/YR-4	221 Elm Street Nita City, Nita	18-10-105 Gambling	Dismissed with leave
3/10/YR-3	221 Elm Street Nita City, Nita	18-10-105 Gambling	Dismissed with leave
8/7/YR-3	221 Elm Street Nita City, Nita	18-10-105 Gambling	Dismissed with leave
12/21/YR-2	221 Elm Street Nita City, Nita	18-10-105 Gambling	Dismissed with leave
5/24/YR-2	221 Elm Street Nita City, Nita	18-10-105 Gambling	Dismissed with leave
9/18/YR-2	221 Elm Street Nita City, Nita	18-10-105 Gambling	Dismissed with leave
4/18/YR-1	221 Elm Street Nita City, Nita	18-10-105 Gambling	Dismissed with leave
12/30/YR-1	221 Elm Street Nita City, Nita	18-10-105 Gambling	Dismissed with leave

UNIFORM ARREST REPORT AND DISPOSITION RECORD (Continued)

NAME: John Burns		DOB: 9/4/YR-35	
SS. NO. 045-38-6262		POB: Meriden, Nita	
DATE	ADDRESS	OFFENSE	DISPOSITION
5/11/YR-0	221 Elm Street Nita City, Nita	18-3-102 (1)(b) Murder 18-6-302 Armed Robbery	Pending

Alexander McConachie
Superintendent of Documents

Certified as of this 13th day of May, YR-0.

Charlotte Noll, Notary Public

STATE OF NITA
DEPARTMENT OF MOTOR VEHICLES

Automobile Registration Division
(721) 555-0600

State House
Nita City, Nita 99990

May 13, YR-0

Detective Arthur Hellman
Nita City Police Department
Nita City, Nita 99990

Dear Detective Hellman:

As you requested during our conversation of May 11, YR-0, this letter is written confirmation of the information given you at that time. John Burns, of 221 Elm Street, Nita City, Nita, is the listed owner of a YR-1, 2-door, green Oldsmobile Cutlass with Nita markers KAM 138.

A certified copy of the registration is attached.

Sincerely,

P. Jones

P. Jones
Division Chief

PJ/ab

Enclosure

STATE OF NITA
DEPARTMENT OF MOTOR VEHICLES

Automobile Registration Division
(721) 555-0600

State House
Nita City, Nita 99990

	LICENSE NO. KAM138		VALIDATION			
OWNER'S COPY Vehicle Reg. Cert.	VALID TO Feb. 15, YR+1		NITA DEPARTMENT OF TRANSPORTATION DIVISION OF MOTOR VEHICLES			
	TITLE NUMBER 17380475	MAKE Olds	STYLE 2 Dr	YR. YR-1	COLOR Gr.	
IMPORTANT: To retain plate, liability insurance must be maintained continuously						
VEHICLE IDENTIFICATION NUMBER E0062EGD14184			TOTAL FEE 15.00			
GROSS WEIGHT	CLASSIFICATION		EQUIP. NO.	STATUS		

MR. JOHN BURNS
221 Elm Street
Nita City, Nita 99993

OWNER'S SIGNATURE

John Burns

The foregoing is a true and accurate copy of the record presently on file in the Department of Motor Vehicles, Automobile Registration Division.

P. Jones

P. Jones, Division Chief

SUBSCRIBED AND SWORN to before me this 13th day of May, YR-0.

Anne Dolan

Notary Public

STATE OF NITA
DEPARTMENT OF PUBLIC SAFETY

Weapons Registration Division
(721) 555-0610

State House
Nita City, Nita 99990

May 12, YR-0

Detective Arthur Hellman
Nita City Police Department
Nita City, Nita 99990

Dear Art:

This letter will confirm our verbal report to you on May 11, YR-0, as to the registration of two pistols presently held by your Department as evidence in a criminal prosecution.

The first weapon, a Smith and Wesson .38, serial no. V 672952, is confirmed as being registered to Mary N. Burns, 221 Elm Street, Nita City, Nita. The other pistol, a Colt .22, serial no. 348X75H 498, is presently registered in the name of James S. Carletti, 61 Hill Avenue, Nita City, Nita. Certified copies of the weapons' registrations are attached.

If I can be of any further assistance to you, please give me a call. Please notify this office when a disposition of these weapons is made.

Sincerely,

W B Cody

W. B. Cody
Division Chief

SBC/db

Encl. (2)

STATE OF NITA
DEPARTMENT OF PUBLIC SAFETY

Weapons Registration Division
(721) 555-0610

State House
Nita City, Nita 99990

Owner's Name: James S. Carletti

Address: 61 Hill Avenue

City/State/Zip: Nita City, Nita 99991

Are you a citizen of the United States? Yes

Have you ever been convicted of a felony? No

Manufacturer of weapons: Colt Arms Co.

Model Type: Pistol

Caliber: .22

Serial No.: 348X75H 498

Has the serial number been changed or altered in any way? No

Date of purchase: 4/12/YR-0

Seller: The Sport Mart

Seller's address: 324 Main Street

Seller's city/state/zip: Nita City, Nita 99993

The foregoing is a true and accurate copy of the original document on file in the offices of the Department of Public Safety, Division of Weapons Registration.

W B Cody

W. B. Cody, Division Chief

SUBSCRIBED AND SWORN TO before me this 11th day of May, YR-1.

Anne Dolan

Notary Public

STATE OF NITA
DEPARTMENT OF PUBLIC SAFETY

Weapons Registration Division
(721) 555-0610

State House
Nita City, Nita 99990

Owner's Name: Mary N. Burns

Address: 221 Elm Street

City/State/Zip: Nita City, Nita 99993

Are you a citizen of the United States? Yes

Have you ever been convicted of a felony? No

Manufacturer of weapons: Smith & Wesson

Model Type: Pistol

Caliber: .38

Serial No.: V 672952

Has the serial number been changed or altered in any way? No

Date of purchase: 8/8/YR-3

Seller: Brown's Pawn Shop

Seller's address: Whitehead Road

Seller's city/state/zip: Nita City, Nita 99992

The foregoing is a true and accurate copy of the original document on file in the offices of the Department of Public Safety, Division of Weapons Registration.

W B Cody

W. B. Cody, Division Chief

SUBSCRIBED AND SWORN TO before me this 11th day of May, YR-0.

Anne Dolan

Notary Public

EXHIBIT — Medical Examiner's Certificate of Death

COPY 1
FOR STATE
VITAL RECORDS

REGISTRATION DISTRICT NO. 07 LOCAL NO. YR-0/248

DIVISION OF HEALTH SERVICES · VITAL RECORDS BRANCH

MEDICAL EXAMINER'S CERTIFICATE OF DEATH

DECEASED

1. NAME OF DECEASED (FIRST / MIDDLE / LAST): Teresa Bianco Carletti
2. SEX: F
3. DATE OF DEATH (MONTH DAY YEAR): May 9, YR-0
4. COLOR OR RACE: White
5a. STATE OF BIRTH (if not in U.S.A. name country): Italy
5b. COUNTY OF BIRTH:
6. DATE OF BIRTH (Month, Day, Year): Jan. 23, YR-55
7. AGE IN YEARS LAST BIRTHDAY: 55 — IF UNDER 1 YEAR: MONTHS / DAYS — IF UNDER 24 HOURS: HOURS / MIN
8a. PLACE OF DEATH COUNTY: Nita
8b. CITY OR TOWN: Nita City
8c. NAME OF HOSPITAL OR INSTITUTION (IF NOT IN EITHER GIVE STREET AND NUMBER): Memorial Hospital
8d. IF HOSP OR INST (Specify DOA, Emer. Rm., Inpatient/O P): DOA
8e. INSIDE CITY LIMITS (SPECIFY YES OR NO): Yes
9a. RESIDENCE—STATE: Nita
9b. COUNTY: Darrow
9c. CITY OR TOWN: Nita City
9d. STREET AND NUMBER OR RFD NO.: 61 Hill Ave.
9e. INSIDE CITY LIMITS (Specify Yes or No): Yes
10. CITIZEN OF WHAT COUNTRY?: U. S.
11. MARRIED, NEVER MARRIED, WIDOWED, DIVORCED (SPECIFY): Married
12. SURVIVING SPOUSE (IF WIFE GIVE MAIDEN NAME): James S. Carletti
13. SOCIAL SECURITY NUMBER: 024-33-3918
14a. USUAL OCCUPATION (KIND OF WORK DONE DURING MOST OF WORKING LIFE, EVEN IF RETIRED): Grocer
14b. KIND OF BUSINESS OR INDUSTRY: Grocery Store
15. WAS DECEDENT EVER IN U S ARMED FORCES? (Specify Yes or No): No
16. FATHER'S NAME: Alphonso Bianco
17. MOTHER'S MAIDEN NAME: Maria LiCalsi
18a. INFORMANT'S NAME AND ADDRESS: James S. Carletti, 61 Hill Ave., Nita City, Nita
18b. RELATION TO DECEASED: Husband

CAUSE

19. PART 1. DEATH CAUSED BY: (ENTER ONLY ONE CAUSE PER LINE FOR (A), (B), (C)) — APPROXIMATE INTERVAL BETWEEN ONSET AND DEATH

(a) IMMEDIATE CAUSE: Cardiac insufficiency

CONDITIONS, IF ANY WHICH GAVE RISE TO IMMEDIATE CAUSE (a), STATING THE UNDERLYING CAUSE LAST.

(b) DUE TO, OR AS A CONSEQUENCE OF: Severed aorta

(c) DUE TO, OR AS A CONSEQUENCE OF: gunshot wound — 5 mins.

20a. PART II. OTHER SIGNIFICANT CONDITIONS (CONTRIBUTING TO DEATH BUT NOT RELATED TO CAUSE GIVEN IN PART I (a)): None
20b. AUTOPSY (SPECIFY) YES OR NO: Yes — ME OR OTHER: Rothman
20c. IF YES WERE FINDINGS CONSIDERED IN DETERMINING CAUSE OF DEATH: Yes
21a. ACCIDENT, SUICIDE, HOMICIDE, UNDETERMINED, NATURAL CAUSES, OR PENDING (SPECIFY): Homicide
21b. DESCRIBE HOW INJURY OCCURED (ENTER NATURE OF INJURY IN PART I OR PART II): Struck by bullet fired at armed holdup man
21c. TIME OF INJURY (MONTH / DAY / YEAR / HOUR): May / 9 / 0 / 4:10 P.M.
21d. INJURY AT WORK (SPECIFY YES OR NO): Yes
21e. PLACE OF INJURY (AT HOME, FARM, STREET, FACTORY, OFFICE BLDG., ETC (SPECIFY)): At store
21f. CITY OR R.F.D. / COUNTY / STATE: Nita City, Nita, Nita

CERTIFIER

MEDICAL EXAMINER CERTIFICATION: ON THE BASIS OF THE EXAMINATION OF THE BODY AND/OR THE INVESTIGATION, IN MY OPINION, DEATH OCCURRED ON THE DATE AND DUE TO THE CAUSE(S) STATED

22a. DEATH OCCURRED (HOUR): 4:15 p.m.
22b. THE DECEDENT WAS PRONOUNCED DEAD (MONTH / DAY / YEAR / HOUR): May / 9 / 0 / 4:28 p.m.
23a. DATE SIGNED (MONTH DAY YEAR): May 10, YR-0
23b. SIGNATURE: Brian Blackbourne
23c. ADDRESS: County Office Building
23d. MEDICAL EXAMINER OF (SPECIFY COUNTY): Darrow

BURIAL

24a. BURIAL, CREMATION, OTHER (SPECIFY): Burial
24b. DATE: May 13
24c. NAME OF CEMETERY OR CREMATORY: Lady of Fatima
24d. LOCATION (CITY, TOWN OR COUNTY) (STATE): Nita City, Nita
25. FUNERAL HOME (NAME / ADDRESS): Belote Mortuary, Nita City, Nita
26. SIGNATURE OF FUNERAL DIRECTOR: Tom Belote — LICENSE NO. 412K6
27a. DATE REC'D BY LOCAL REG.: 5/13/YR-0
27b. SIGNATURE OF REGISTRAR: Adrienne Fox
28. SIGNATURE OF EMBALMER (IF EMBALMED): Tom Belote — LICENSE NO. 18921

MEDICAL EXAMINER: After you have initiated the Certificate of Death, give copies 1 & 3 to funeral director when body is released, and route copy 2 to Chief Medical Examiner. If cause of death is pending, file Supplemental Report of Cause of Death (Form VS 8A) when the additional information has been obtained.
FUNERAL DIRECTOR: Copy 1 must be completed and filed with the Local Registrar within 5 days after Death. Copy 3, when signed by the medical examiner is your authorization for final disposition.

DHS FORM 2164
REV 1/78

STATEMENT OF JOHN BURNS**

My name is John Burns and I was born on September 4, YR-35, in Meriden, Nita. I have a high school education. I understand that I have a right not to talk and have a lawyer, but I haven't done anything wrong so I want to give this statement and I don't need a lawyer.

I went into the Army a year after high school and was in until I got a medical discharge because I became addicted to heroin while I was in Germany. After I got out I came back to Nita City. I wasn't able to find a job. Shortly after I got home, I was arrested for having some heroin. It was true so I pleaded guilty. I got 2 to 5 years. I served a little over a year at the Nita State Prison. I was arrested once more for using heroin in December of YR-9. My lawyer made a deal and I went back for 11 more months.

When I got out I was off dope and I haven't used any since. I married my wife, Mary, about eight years ago. We have three kids: John, Jr., 6; David, 4; and Patsy, 3.

Right after the wedding I got a job as a bartender at the White Swan Bar. I had that job until about six months ago when the owner sold it and they turned it into another steak and salad place. When I was laid off I was making a little over $200 a week between tips and salary. Right now I'm drawing $81.50 a week in unemployment and my wife works by taking care of the neighbors' kids while their parents work. She makes between $80 and $120 each week.

We keep six guns in our house. My wife owns them because I have a record and can't get a license for them. I removed the firing pins from all of them for the safety of the kids. We keep no ammunition in the house. We have two Remington .22 long barrel rifles, a Winchester 20-20 shot gun, two Mauser pistols I got in Germany, and a Smith and Wesson .38 I bought several years ago from Brown's Pawn Shop.

About a week before I was arrested, I noticed the .38 pistol was missing from the gun cabinet in the living room which is always unlocked. Neither Mary nor the kids had seen it. I told Mary to report it. For about a week I bugged Mary to call the police. She finally did it this morning. If she had done it when I told her to take care of it, none of this would have happened to me.

**This statement was given to Detective Arthur Hellman at the Nita City Police Station immediately after John Burns was arrested.

We do have some money problems because I'm unemployed. Patsy, our daughter, needs an operation and we can't afford it. But, the house we live in is ours, free and clear. We can get a mortgage on it if we need money to pay for the operation.

On Saturday, May 9, YR-0, I was home all day except for about an hour and a half in the morning when I went to the King Soopers Market to do the marketing. I have never shopped or even been in Carletti's IGA. Larry Roberts was coming over in the afternoon to watch the Las Vegas Invitational Bowling Tournament on television.

Larry is a guy I bowl with Tuesday nights in a league. We both belong to the Knights of Columbus and we met about five years ago at one of their meetings. He's also an insurance agent and I have a policy with him. As a matter of fact, he has loaned me money to make the last couple of payments on the policy, as I've been short of cash. I've always been honest with him. He knows all about my criminal record.

A little after three, I think it was, Larry called to tell me his work was more than he expected and that he wouldn't be over until about 4:30. I gave him a hard time about working too hard, but told him I would see him then. That's all I remember about the phone conversation. Mary was in the kitchen while I was on the phone with Larry. As a matter of fact, she had answered the phone.

After I got off the phone, I went back inside and sat down in front of the television and drank some beer. I was really tired. I had been working around the house all day. I had cleaned out all of the gutters and turned the television antenna to get the best possible reception on Channel 8 which carried the bowling.

Mary went downstairs after the phone call. She was doing all the laundry. I could hear the machines while I was watching the Red Sox-Yankees game on television. I never left the house between 3:30 and 4:30.

Larry arrived at 4:30. I filled him in on what had happened in the first frames and then we watched the rest of the bowling tournament. I think he left about 6:00.

Sunday was Mother's Day and the kids and I took Mary her breakfast in bed. We spent the entire day around the house. Monday I went out looking for jobs again. I went to the State Employment Service to pick up my check and get some new leads. They only had two for me. One job was at a bar in Nita City and the other was a dishwashing job in Meriden. Both jobs were taken by the time I got there.

I went home at about 4:30. Just after we sat down to dinner at about 6:30, the doorbell rang. Mary went to answer it. She called for me. I came to the door and a police officer was standing there. I said, "What is it this time, officer, another gambling roust?" They've been harassing me for the last five years. I don't know why. They keep arresting me for gambling and letting me go. The officer said, "This time you blew it, the charge is Murder One." I couldn't believe it. Mary started to cry. The officer put handcuffs on me and they took me downtown. I think the kids were scared to death.

NAME: John Burns

DATE: May 11, YR-0

SUBSCRIBED AND SWORN TO before me this 11th day of May, YR-0.

Katty M. Kennedy
Notary Public

CONFIDENTIAL

ATTORNEY WORK PRODUCT

TO: Defense Counsel

FROM: B. Ross, Investigator BR

DATE: 5/20/YR-0

RE: INTERVIEW WITH JOHN BURNS

Pursuant to your request, I went to see John Burns in the County Jail and interviewed him. In response to questioning about his knowledge of Lauren Jones, he indicated that he did know Jones. They apparently met while in prison about nine years ago. Burns indicates they were not friends; Jones was someone he said hello to and nothing more. Burns says he had few friends in prison and that he was "just doing time." They were both in the same cell block for several months. He does admit that his nickname in prison was "Burnsey."

I asked Burns when he last saw Jones. Burns indicated that their last meeting was while they were still in prison. He says he did not know Jones was still in the state. Burns emphatically denies participation in the Carletti robbery and says he never left his house that afternoon.

Burns indicated to me that he knows where McSorley's is located and has been there on one or two occasions. He insists, however, that he has never been there with Jones and, in fact, has not been there within the last two years.

STATEMENT OF MARY N. BURNS**

My name is Mary N. Burns and I am 33 years old. I have been married to John Burns for 8 years. We have three children. They are John, Jr., 6; David, 4; and Patsy, 3. We live at 221 Elm Street in Nita City in a house that my father left to us when he died. It is a small house, seven rooms, but we got it free and clear and not having a mortgage is really nice when your husband is out of work.

When I married John, he had just gotten out of prison after serving two terms for using heroin. He had the drugs because when he came back from the Army, he was an addict. He wanted me to marry him just before he was arrested, but I wouldn't do it because I didn't want my babies to be born sick. After he got out of prison, he stayed clean. I've loved him ever since high school, so when he got out of prison and stayed off drugs, I married him. He has never used any drugs since.

John has been arrested several times since we got married. I think each time it's been for gambling. John doesn't gamble. We never had enough money for him to be able to afford to do that. I don't know why the police keep harassing him. I guess every time a crime is committed, they assume John did it just because he went to jail once before.

John is a good provider. Until he lost his job as a bartender at the White Swan, we never had any money problems. He was making about $200 a week. He always handled the finances and while we never had much money, we always had enough. When he lost his job, everything started to go wrong.

Patsy got sick and now the doctors tell us she needs an expensive operation. She has something wrong with her small intestine. That's why John goes out every day and tries to find work. He's trying so hard, but with so many people out of work, it's really hard. Now that this has happened, I don't know if anyone will hire him.

I've been trying to help out by taking in some of the neighbors' kids on weekdays. Their mothers have jobs and they pay me $40 per week for each kid. Usually, I get three kids. John gets about $80 a week from unemployment.

John has a gun collection. Some are guns he brought back from when he was stationed in Germany with the Army. The others he bought here in Nita City. The guns are registered in my name

**This statement was given to Detective Arthur Hellman at the Nita City Police Station the morning following John Burns's arrest.

because John says there is some law that says that anyone who has been in prison can't own a gun. I think there were six guns; three pistols, two rifles, and a shotgun.

The first weekend in May, on Saturday, John and I took the kids to the Nita City Zoo. When we got home, John noticed that one of the guns was missing. He asked me if I knew where the gun was and I said I hadn't seen it since Thursday when I dusted. The missing gun was a pistol. I don't know enough about guns to know what kind it was. I asked the kids if they had seen the gun and they said no. John said I should report it missing to the police the first thing on Monday morning. All the next week John kept bugging me to call the police, but I never got around to doing it until yesterday morning.

We don't lock the gun cabinet because the guns are only for decoration. John never uses any of them and all the firing pins had been removed. We keep no bullets for any of the guns in the house.

John usually stays around the house on weekends as I'm really tired and I need help with the kids. On Saturday, May 9, YR-0, Mrs. Womble, who lives next door, took my kids for the entire day. I take care of her child, Dana, during the week because Mrs. Womble works as a phone installer. That Saturday, Mrs. Womble came over in the morning and said as a Mother's Day present to me, she was going to take my kids for the entire day.

John and I were alone in the house all day. It was so quiet, a beautiful warm sunny day. In the morning, John went to the store and did all the marketing for the week. We always shop at King Soopers. We have never shopped at Carletti's IGA. I straightened up around the house and collected all the kids' dirty laundry. I wanted to make the house look good because John told me that Larry Roberts was coming over in the afternoon to watch bowling on television.

Larry called at about 3:30 and asked to speak to John. I was in the kitchen at the time sorting the white and dark loads for the washing machine. I only heard one side of the conversation, but it sounded like Larry told John he was going to come over late.

I started downstairs to the laundry room just after John hung up the phone. I told John I would be in the basement for a while doing the wash and ironing his shirts. He said he would yell down if he needed anything.

The laundry room is in the basement. It has two windows just below the ceiling which look out at about ground level on the driveway, which is cement. John's green Oldsmobile was in the carport.

I stayed in the basement doing the laundry until about 5:00. During the entire time I was downstairs, I did not hear John leave. When I came upstairs, John and Larry were sitting in the living room watching bowling and drinking beer. Larry left just before dinner, which was at 6:30, just like it is every day.

During the entire time I was downstairs, I heard the television, even though the washer and dryer were on. I never saw or heard the car pull out of the driveway. I wasn't looking out the window all the time, but I think I would have heard or seen the car pull out if John had gone anywhere.

On Monday, May 11, YR-0, just as I was serving dinner to John and the kids, the doorbell rang. I opened the door and a man was standing there. He told me his name (I forget what it was) and showed me his police badge. He asked me if my husband was home. When I said he was, he asked if I would get him. John came to the door and the officer asked him if he was John Burns. The officer handed him a piece of paper and told him he was under arrest for murder. I couldn't believe it. They took him away and he's been in jail ever since.

NAME: Mary Burns

DATE: May 12, YR-0

SUBSCRIBED AND SWORN TO before me this 12th day of May, YR-0.

Kathy M. Kennedy
Notary Public

STATEMENT OF LAURENCE R. ROBERTS**

My name is Laurence R. Roberts. My friends call me Larry. I am 38 years old and I live at 32 Stony Brook Road in Nita City, Nita. I work as a salesman for Mutual of Omaha Insurance Company. I have had the job for about three years. Before that, I did construction work until the building boom ended. When that happened, I went back to school and finished college at night at Nita City Community College.

I belong to the Knights of Columbus in Nita City. I first met John Burns at one of their functions about five years ago. We became good friends. I know he did some time in jail for using drugs, but that was a long time ago. He's a new man. He would never do anything illegal now. I know he has been arrested several times since then. I don't know why someone in the police department thinks that every time any kind of crime is committed in Nita City, John is the one who did it. He's paid his debt to society and gone straight. If he was still doing anything illegal, I wouldn't have anything to do with him.

John Burns bought a life insurance policy from me several years ago. He's the kind of client every insurance salesman wants. Until he was laid off, he always paid his premiums on time. The last few months I've been helping him out by advancing the premiums. I know that the Insurance Salesman's Association says it is unethical to advance premiums to a client. It's not illegal and I've never done it before. I'm only doing it now because John is a good friend and I trust him completely.

John and I belong to the Tuesday Night Bowling League over at Westbury Lanes. John is an excellent bowler and has about a 190 average. He usually does well enough to keep our team in the running despite my lousy bowling.

On Saturday afternoon, May 9, YR-0, I was supposed to meet John at his house at 4:00 p.m. to watch the Las Vegas Invitational Bowling Tournament, which was being carried on ABC's Wide World of Sports. Earlier that afternoon, I was at my office working because I was four days past the end of the month and I needed to get my monthly report finished and mailed to the main office. At about 3:15, I realized I would not be able to get my work done and get to John's house by 4:00. I called John's number. Mary answered, and I said hello and asked her to put John on. I told him I was going to be late, and he told me I worked too hard and he was running out of beer. I laughed and told him I

**This statement was given to Detective Arthur Hellman at the Nita City Police Station.

would be over by 4:30 and that I would bring some extra beer. He he would be there and jokingly he added that I shouldn't worry if he wasn't home when he got there. He said if the beer ran out before I got there, he might run out and get a couple of six packs.

I went back to work. When I looked at my watch again, it was a few minutes before 4:30. I walked out to my car and drove to the 7-Eleven store, which is a block from my office. I picked up two six packs of beer, got into my car, and drove directly to John's. His house is less than a mile from the store where I bought the beer. I pulled into his driveway and parked right behind his car, which was in the carport. It was probably 4:40 p.m.

When I got there, John was sitting in his chair watching the television. I stayed at his house until after bowling was over at 6:00. While I was in the house, John never left.

NAME: Laurence Roberts

DATE: May 12, YR-0

SUBSCRIBED AND SWORN TO before me this 12th day of May, YR-0.

Katty McKennedy
Notary Public

APPLICABLE NITA STATUTES

NITA Criminal Code--Chapter 40

Section 18-3-102. Murder in the First Degree

(1) A person commits the crime of murder in the first degree if:

(a) With premeditated intent to cause the death of a person other than himself, he causes the death of that person or of another person; or

(b) Acting either alone or with one or more persons, he commits or attempts to com- mit arson, robbery, burglary, kidnapping, rape, or any sexual offense prohibited by sections 18-3-402 through 18-3-404, and in the course of or in furtherance of the crime that he is committing or attempting to commit, or the immediate flight therefrom, the death of a person, other than one of the participants, is caused.

(2) Murder in the first degree is a class 1 felony.

Section 18-6-301. Robbery

(1) A person or one with whom he participates who takes anything of value from the person or presence of another by the use of force, threats, or intimidation commits robbery.

(2) Robbery is a class 4 felony.

Section 18-6-302. Armed Robbery

(1) A person who uses a deadly weapon in committing a robbery commits armed robbery.

(2) Armed robbery is a class 3 felony.

Section 18-2-101. Definitions

(4) Deadly weapon. A deadly weapon is any thing or instrument which may be used to cause serious bodily injury or death.

Section 18-1-105. Felonies Classified — Penalties

(1) Felonies are divided into five classes, which are distinguished from one another by the following penalties which are authorized upon conviction:

Class	Minimum Sentence	Maximum Sentence
1	Life imprisonment	Life imprisonment
2	Ten years imprisonment	Fifty years imprisonment
3	Five years imprisonment	Forty years imprisonment
4	One year imprisonment, or two thousand dollars fine	Ten years imprisonment, thirty thousand dollars fine, or both
5	One year imprisonment, or one thousand dollars fine	Five years imprisonment, fifteen thousand dollars fine, or both

APPLICABLE NITA CASE LAW

Rulings of the Nita Supreme Court

1. In the State of Nita, the Supreme Court has held that a gun unloaded or incapable of firing is per se a deadly weapon.

2. The Nita Supreme Court recently considered the question of whether a participant in the commission of one of the felonies enumerated in 18-3-102(1)(b) can be convicted of felony murder where one non-participant is killed by another non-participant resisting the felony. It ruled that a conviction under those circumstances is within the intent of the statute.

PROPOSED JURY INSTRUCTIONS**

1. The Court will now instruct you on the law governing this case. You must arrive at your verdict by unanimous vote applying the law, as you are now instructed, to the facts as you find them to be.

2. The State of Nita has charged the defendant, John Burns, with the crimes of Armed Robbery and First Degree Murder.

3. Under the criminal code of the State of Nita, a person commits the crime of Armed Robbery if he, or one with whom he participates, takes anything of value from the person or presence of another by the use of force, threats or intimidation, and a deadly weapon.

4. To sustain the charge of Armed Robbery, the State must prove the following propositions:

   (a) That defendant, or one with whom he participated, took something;

   (b) That the thing taken was of value;

   (c) That the thing taken was from the person or presence of another; and

   (d) That the thing was taken by the use of force, threats or intimidation, and a deadly weapon.

   I instruct you that under the law of the State of Nita a real gun, whether capable of firing or not, is a deadly weapon.

   If you find from your consideration of all the evidence that each of these propositions has been proved beyond a reasonable doubt, then you should find the defendant guilty of Armed Robbery.

   If, on the other hand, you find from your consideration of all the evidence that any of these propositions has not been proved beyond a reasonable doubt, then you should find the defendant not guilty of Armed Robbery.

**These proposed instructions are those applicable to this case only. For general instructions, see those set forth after these instructions.

5. Under the criminal code of the State of Nita, a person commits the crime of First Degree Murder if:

   (a) Acting either alone or with one or more persons, he commits or attempts to commit the crime of Armed Robbery; and

   (b) In the course of or in furtherance of the crime, or the immediate flight therefrom, the death of a person, other than one of the participants, is caused.

6. To sustain the charge of First Degree Murder, the State must prove the following propositions:

   (a) That defendant acting with one or more persons committed, or attempted to commit, the crime of Armed Robbery; and

   (b) That in the course of or in the furtherance of that Armed Robbery, or the immediate flight therefrom, the death of Teresa Carletti was caused.

   If you find from your consideration of all the evidence that each of these propositions has been proved beyond a reasonable doubt, then you should find the defendant guilty of First Degree Murder.

   If, on the other hand, you find from your consideration of all the evidence that any of these propositions has not been proved beyond a reasonable doubt, then you should find the defendant not guilty of First Degree Murder.

7. Proximate Cause. The death of Teresa Carletti must have been proximately caused by the conduct of defendant, or someone acting in concert or in partnership with defendant.

   Proximate cause means that cause which in its natural and probable sequence produced the death of the victim, Mrs. Carletti. It is the cause without which the death would not have occurred.

   If you find that the death of Teresa Carletti was not proximately caused by the defendant's conduct, or the conduct of one acting in concert or in partnership with the defendant, or if you have a reasonable doubt with respect thereto, then your verdict must be not guilty.

NITA
GENERAL JURY INSTRUCTIONS

The following jury instructions are intended for use with any of the files contained in these materials regardless of whether the trial is in Nita state court or in federal court. In addition, each of the files contains special instructions dealing with the law applicable in the particular case. The instructions set forth here state general principles that may be applicable in any of the cases and may be used at the discretion of the trial judge.***

PART I. PRELIMINARY INSTRUCTIONS GIVEN PRIOR TO THE EVIDENCE (For Civil or Criminal Cases)

Nita Instruction 01:01--Introduction

You have been selected as jurors and have taken an oath to well and truly try this cause. This trial will last one day.

During the progress of the trial there will be periods of time when the Court recesses. During those periods of time, you must not talk about this case among yourselves or with anyone else.

During the trial, do not talk to any of the parties, their lawyers or any of the witnesses.

If any attempt is made by anyone to talk to you concerning the matters here under consideration, you should immediately report that fact to the Court.

You should keep an open mind. You should not form or express an opinion during the trial and should reach no conclusion in this case until you have heard all of the evidence, the arguments of counsel, and the final instructions as to the law that will be given to you by the Court.

Nita Instruction 01:02--Conduct of the Trial

First, the attorneys will have an opportunity to make opening statements. These statements are not evidence and should be considered only as a preview of what the attorneys expect the evidence will be.

***The instructions contained in this section are borrowed or adapted from a number of sources including California, Illinois, Indiana, Washington and Colorado Pattern Jury Instructions.

Following the opening statements, witnesses will be called to testify. They will be placed under oath and questioned by the attorneys. Documents and other tangible exhibits may also be received as evidence. If an exhibit is given to you to examine, you should examine it carefully, individually, and without any comment.

It is counsel's right and duty to object when testimony or other evidence is being offered that he or she believes is not admissible.

When the Court sustains an objection to a question, the jurors must disregard the question and the answer, if one has been given, and draw no inference from the question or answer or speculate as to what the witness would have said if permitted to answer. Jurors must also disregard evidence stricken from the record.

When the Court sustains an objection to any evidence the jurors must disregard that evidence.

When the Court overrules an objection to any evidence, the jurors must not give that evidence any more weight than if the objection had not been made.

When the evidence is completed, the attorneys will make final statements. These final statements are not evidence but are given to assist you in evaluating the evidence. The attorneys are also permitted to argue in an attempt to persuade you to a particular verdict. You may accept or reject those arguments as you see fit.

Finally, just before you retire to consider your verdict, I will give you further instructions on the law that applies to this case.

PART II. FINAL INSTRUCTIONS
GENERAL PRINCIPLES

General Instructions for Both Civil and Criminal Cases

Nita Instruction 1:01--Introduction

Members of the jury, the evidence and arguments in this case have been completed, and I will now instruct you as to the law.

The law applicable to this case is stated in these instructions and it is your duty to follow all of them. You must not single out certain instructions and disregard others.

It is your duty to determine the facts, and to determine them only from the evidence in this case. You are to apply the law to the facts and in this way decide the case. You must not be governed or influenced by sympathy or prejudice for or against any party in this case. Your verdict must be based on evidence and not upon speculation, guess, or conjecture.

From time to time the court has ruled on the admissibility of evidence. You must not concern yourselves with the reasons for these rulings. You should disregard questions and exhibits that were withdrawn or to which objections were sustained.

You should also disregard testimony and exhibits that the court has refused or stricken.

The evidence that you should consider consists only of the witnesses' testimonies and the exhibits the court has received.

Any evidence that was received for a limited purpose should not be considered by you for any other purpose.

You should consider all the evidence in the light of your own observations and experiences in life.

Neither by these instructions nor by any ruling or remark that I have made do I mean to indicate any opinion as to the facts or as to what your verdict should be.

Nita Instruction 1:02--Opening Statements and Closing Arguments

Opening statements are made by the attorneys to acquaint you with the facts they expect to prove. Closing arguments are made by the attorneys to discuss the facts and circumstances in the case, and should be confined to the evidence and to reasonable inferences to be drawn therefrom. Neither opening statements nor closing arguments are evidence, and any statement or argument made by the attorneys that is not based on the evidence should be disregarded.

Nita Instruction 1:03--Credibility of Witnesses

You are the sole judges of the credibility of the witnesses and of the weight to be given to the testimony of each witness. In determining what credit is to be given any witness, you may take into account his ability and opportunity to observe; his manner and appearance while testifying; any interest, bias, or prejudice he may have; the reasonableness of his testimony considered in the light of all the evidence; and any other factors that bear on the believability and weight of the witness's testimony.

Nita Instruction 1:04--Expert Witnesses

You have heard evidence in this case from witnesses who testified as experts. The law allows experts to express an opinion on subjects involving their special knowledge, training and skill, experience, or research. While their opinions are allowed to be given, it is entirely within the province of the jury to determine what weight shall be given their testimony. Jurors are not bound by the testimony of experts; their testimony is to be weighed as that of any other witness.

Nita Instruction 1:05--Direct and Circumstantial Evidence

The law recognizes two kinds of evidence: direct and circumstantial. Direct evidence proves a fact directly; that is, the evidence by itself, if true, establishes the fact. Circumstantial evidence is the proof of facts or circumstances that give rise to a reasonable inference of other facts; that is, circumstantial evidence proves a fact indirectly in that it follows from other facts or circumstances according to common experience and observations in life. An eyewitness is a common example of direct evidence, while human footprints are circumstantial evidence that a person was present.

The law makes no distinction between direct and circumstantial evidence as to the degree or amount of proof required, and each should be considered according to whatever weight or value it may have. All of the evidence should be considered and evaluated by you in arriving at your verdict.

Nita Instruction 1:06--Concluding Instruction

The Court did not in any way and does not by these instructions give or intimate any opinions as to what has or has not been proven in the case, or as to what are or are not the facts of the case.

No one of these instructions states all of the law applicable, but all of them must be taken, read, and considered together as they are connected with and related to each other as a whole.

You must not be concerned with the wisdom of any rule of law. Regardless of any opinions you may have as to what the law ought to be, it would be a violation of your sworn duty to base a verdict upon any other view of the law than that given in the instructions of the court.

General Instructions for Civil Cases Only

Nita Instruction 2:01--Burden of Proof

When I say that a party has the burden of proof on any issue, or use the expression "if you find," "if you decide," or "by a preponderance of the evidence," I mean that you must be persuaded from a consideration of all the evidence in the case that the issue in question is more probably true than not true.

Any findings of fact you make must be based on probabilities, not possibilities. It may not be based on surmise, speculation, or conjecture.

Nita Instruction 2:02--Corporate Party

One [Both] of the parties in this case is a corporation [are corporations], and it is [they are] entitled to the same fair treatment as an individual would be entitled to under like circumstances, and you should decide the case with the same impartiality you would use in deciding a case between individuals.

General Instructions for Criminal Cases Only

Nita Instruction 3:01--Indictment [Information]

The indictment [information] in this case is the formal method of accusing the defendant of a crime and placing him on trial. It is not any evidence against the defendant and does not create any inference of guilt. The [State] [Government] has the burden of proving beyond a reasonable doubt every essential element of the crime charged in the indictment [information] [or any of the crimes included therein].

Nita Instruction 3:02--Burden of Proof

The [State] [Government] has the burden of proving the guilt of the defendant beyond a reasonable doubt, and this burden remains on the [State] [Government] throughout the case. The defendant is not required to prove his innocence.

Nita Instruction 3:03--Reasonable Doubt

Reasonable doubt means a doubt based upon reason and common sense that arises from a fair and rational consideration of all the evidence or lack of evidence in the case. It is a doubt that is not a vague, speculative, or imaginary doubt, but such a doubt as would cause reasonable persons to hesitate to act in matters of importance to themselves.

Nita Instruction 3:04--Presumption of Innocence

The defendant is presumed to be innocent of the charges against him. This presumption remains with him throughout every stage of the trial and during your deliberations on the verdict. The presumption is not overcome until, from all the evidence in the case, you are convinced beyond a reasonable doubt that the defendant is guilty.

Nita Instruction 3:05--Reputation/Character

The defendant has introduced evidence of his character and reputation for [truth and veracity] [being a peaceful and law-abiding citizen] [morality] [chastity] [honesty and integrity] [etc.]. This evidence may be sufficient when considered with the other evidence in the case to raise a reasonable doubt of the defendant's guilt. However, if from all the evidence in the case you are satisfied beyond a reasonable doubt of the defendant's guilt, then it is your duty to find him guilty, even though he may have a good reputation for ____________________________.

IN THE SUPERIOR COURT OF
DARROW COUNTY
STATE OF NITA

THE PEOPLE OF THE STATE OF NITA vs. JOHN BURNS, Defendant.	)))))))	 Case No. CR 324 JURY VERDICT

We, the Jury, return the following verdict, and each of us concurs in this verdict:

[Choose the appropriate verdict]

I. ARMED ROBBERY

We, the Jury, find the defendant, John Burns, NOT GUILTY of Armed Robbery.

____
Foreperson

We, the Jury, find the defendant, John Burns, GUILTY of Armed Robbery.

____
Foreperson

If, and only if, you find the defendant guilty of Armed Robbery, then you must consider the additional charge of Murder in the First Degree.

II. MURDER IN THE FIRST DEGREE

We, the Jury, find the Defendant, John Burns, NOT GUILTY of Murder in the First Degree.

____
Foreperson

We, the Jury, find the Defendant, John Burns, GUILTY of Murder in the First Degree.

____
Foreperson